S0-CEW-945

A
CURRENCY
of
HPE

A
CURRENCY
of
HPE

Copyright 1999

by Debtors Anonymous General Service Board, Inc.

All Rights Reserved

First Printing, April 1999

Debtors Anonymous General Service Conference Approved

Debtors Anonymous, D.A., and the D.A. logo are registered trademarks™
of
Debtors Anonymous General Service Board, Inc.

Debtors Anonymous
General Service Office
P.O. Box 920888
Needham, MA 02492-0009
(781) 453-2743
(800) 421-2383
www.debtorsanonymous.org

Printed in the United States of America

Table of Contents

Our Stories

PASS IT ON

FOREWORD

We, the men and women of Debtors Anonymous, come together to solve our common problem of compulsive debting. We share our experience, strength and hope with one another to arrest the disease of debting. We have found compulsive debting to be a painful, confusing and destructive disorder. Compulsive debting takes many forms from incurring unsecured debt to compulsive shopping, from grandiose thinking to deprivation mentality. All these symptoms of debting seriously affect our *quality of life–financially, emotionally, mentally, spiritually, physically and socially.*

As members of Debtors Anonymous, we have chosen a *spiritual path* of healing and growth which requires working the "Twelve Steps" and using the "Twelve Tools of DA." The Twelve Steps form the foundation for our recovery. The D.A. Tools aid us in working the Steps. As a result of beginning this recovery process, we have been able to stop incurring new unsecured debt, one day at a time, and to retire our existing debt through reasonable debt repayment within our means. We are learning to understand ourselves and form genuine loving connections with others and discover a relationship with a Higher Power of our own choice.

We have created this recovery book to share our Program with other compulsive debtors so that they might understand what we have come to know about debting and experience the relief we have found. The stories we have gathered are a collection of members' experiences with debting which share: *"What it was like for them, What happened, How they changed, and What it is like now."* These stories express the opinions and experiences of the individual member and not necessarily those of Debtors Anonymous as a whole.

We hope that if you identify with some, or all, aspects of compulsive debting, you will join us on the path of recovery from compulsive debting and find the peace, joy, hope and love that is here for you.

PREAMBLE OF DEBTORS ANONYMOUS

Debtors Anonymous is a fellowship of men and women who share their experience, strength and hope with each other that they may solve their common problem and help others to recover from compulsive debting. The only requirement for membership is a desire to stop incurring unsecured debt. There are no dues or fees for D.A. membership; we are self-supporting through our own contributions. D.A. is not allied with any sect, denomination, politics, organization or institution; does not wish to engage in any controversy; neither endorses nor opposes any causes. Our primary purpose is to stop debting one day at a time and to help other compulsive debtors to stop incurring unsecured debt.

The Twelve Steps of Debtors Anonymous

1. We admitted we were powerless over debt—that our lives had become unmanageable.

2. Came to believe that a Power greater than ourselves could restore us to sanity.

3. Made a decision to turn our will and our lives over to the care of God *as we understood Him.*

4. Made a searching and fearless moral inventory of ourselves.

5. Admitted to God, to ourselves, and to another human being the exact nature of our wrongs.

6. Were entirely ready to have God remove all these defects of character.

7. Humbly asked Him to remove our shortcomings.

8. Made a list of all persons we had harmed and became willing to made amends to them all.

9. Made direct amends to such people wherever possible, except when to do so would injure them or others.

10. Continued to take personal inventory and when we were wrong, promptly admitted it.

11. Sought through prayer and meditation to improve our conscious contact with God *as we understood Him,* praying only for knowledge of His will for us and the power to carry that out.

12. Having had a spiritual awakening as the result of these steps, we tried to carry this message to compulsive debtors, and to practice these principles in all our affairs.

The Twelve Traditions of Debtors Anonymous

1. Our common welfare should come first; personal recovery depends upon D.A. unity.

2. For our group purpose there is but one ultimate authority—a loving God as He may express Himself in our group conscience. Our leaders are but trusted servants; they do not govern.

3. The only requirement for D.A. membership is a desire to stop incurring unsecured debt.

4. Each group should be autonomous except in matters affecting other groups or D.A. as a whole.

5. Each group has but one primary purpose—to carry its message to the debtor who still suffers.

6. A D.A. group ought never endorse, finance, or lend the D.A. name to any related facility or outside enterprise, lest problems of money, property, or prestige divert us from our primary purpose.

7. Every D.A. group ought to be fully self-supporting, declining outside contributions.

8. Debtors Anonymous should remain forever non-professional, but our service centers may employ special workers.

9. D.A. as such, ought never be organized; but we may create service boards or committees directly responsible to those they serve.

10. Debtors Anonymous has no opinion on outside issues; hence the D.A. name ought never be drawn into public controversy.

11. Our public relations policy is based on attraction rather than promotion; we need always maintain personal anonymity at the level of press, radio, and films.

12. Anonymity is the spiritual foundation of all our traditions, ever reminding us to place principles before personalities.

Signs of Compulsive Debting

1. Being unclear about your financial situation. Not knowing account balances, monthly expenses, loan interest rates, fee, fines, or contractual obligations.

2. Frequently "borrowing" items such as books, pens, or small amounts of money from friends and others, and failing to return them.

3. Poor saving habits. Not planning for taxes, retirement or other not-recurring but predictable items, and then feeling surprised when they come due; a "live for today, don't worry about tomorrow" attitude.

4. Compulsive shopping: Being unable to pass up a "good deal"; making impulsive purchases; leaving price tags on clothes so they can be returned; not using items you've purchased.

5. Difficulty in meeting basic finacial or personal obligations, and/or an inordinate sense of accomplishment when such obligations are met.

6. A different feeling when buying things on credit than when paying cash, a feeling of being in the club, of being accepted, of being grown up.

7. Living in chaos and drama around money: Using one credit card to pay another; bouncing checks; always having a finacial crisis to contend with.

8. A tendency to live on the edge: Living paycheck to paycheck; taking risks with health and car insurance coverage; writing checks hoping money will appear to cover them.

9. Unwarranted inhibition and embarrassment in what should be a normal discussion of money.

10. Overworking or under earning: Working extra hours to earn money to pay creditors; using time inefficiently; taking jobs below your skill and education level.

11. An unwillingness to care for and value yourself: Living in self-imposed deprivation; denying your basic needs in order to pay your creditors.

12. A feeling or hope that someone will take care of you if necessary, so that you won't really get into serious financial trouble, that there will always be someone you can turn to.

The Twelve Tools of Debtors Anonymous

Recovery from compulsive debting begins when we stop incurring new, unsecured debt, one day at a time. (Unsecured debt is any debt that is not backed up by some form of collateral, such as a house or other asset.) We attain a daily reprieve from compulsive debting by practicing the Twelve Steps and by using the following Tools.

1. Meetings

We attend meetings at which we share our experience, strength and hope with one another. Unless we give to newcomers what we have received from D.A., we cannot keep it ourselves.

2. Record Maintenance

We maintain records of our daily income and expenses, of our savings, and of the retirement of any portions of our outstanding debts.

3. Sponsorship

We have found it essential to our recovery to have a sponsor and to be a sponsor. A sponsor is a recovering debtor who guides us through the Twelve Steps and shares his or her own experience, strength, and recovery.

4. Pressure Relief Groups and Pressure Relief Meetings

After we have gained some familiarity with the D.A. program, we organize Pressure Relief Groups consisting of ourselves and two other recovering debtors who have not incurred unsecured debt for at least 90 days and who usually have more experience in the program. The group meets in a series of Pressure Relief Meetings to review our financial situation. These meetings typically result in the formulation of a spending plan and an action plan.

5. Spending Plan

The spending plan puts our needs first and gives us clarity and balance in our spending. It includes categories for income, spending, debt payment and savings (to help us build cash reserves, however humble). The income plan helps us focus on increasing our income. The debt payment category guides us in making realist payment arrangements without depriving ourselves. Savings can include prudent reserve, retirement and special purchases.

6. Action Plan

With the help of our Pressure Relief Group, we develop a list of specific actions for resolving our debts, improving our financial situation, and achieving our goals without incurring unsecured debt.

7. The Telephone and the Internet

We maintain frequent contact with other D.A. members by using the telephone, e-mail, and other forms of communication. We make a point of talking to other D.A. members before and after taking difficult steps in our recovery.

8. D.A. and A.A. Literature

We study the literature of Debtors Anonymous and of Alcoholics Anonymous to strengthen our understanding of compulsive disease and of recovery from compulsive debting. In. A.A. literature we can identify with many of the situations described by substituting the words "compulsive debt" for "alcohol."

9. Awareness

We maintain awareness of the danger of compulsive debt by taking note of the bank, loan company and credit card advertising and their effects on us. We also remain aware of our personal finances in order to avoid vagueness, which can lead to compulsive debting or spending.

10. Business Meetings

We attend business meetings that are held monthly. Many of us have long harbored feelings that "business" was not a part of our lives but for others more qualified. Yet participation in running our own program teaches us how our organization operates, and also helps us to become responsible for our own recovery.

11. Service

We perform service at every level: personal, meeting, Intergroup, and World Service. Service is vital to our recovery. Only through service can we give to others what so generously has been given to us.

12. Anonymity

We practice anonymity, which allows us freedom of expression by assuring us that what we say at meetings or to other D.A .members at any time will not be repeated.

Questions and Answers about Debtors Anonymous

What Is Compulsive Debting?

Compulsive debting is a disease.

We have found that it is a disease that never gets better, only worse, as time goes on. It is a disease, progressive in its nature, which can never be cured but can be arrested.

Before coming to D.A., many compulsive debtors thought of themselves as irresponsible, morally weak, or—at times—just plain "no good." The D.A. concept is that the compulsive debtor is really a very sick person who can recover if he or she will follow, to the best of his or her ability, a simple program that has proved successful for other men and women with a similar problem.

As compulsive debtors, we have fallen into patterns of spending that do not satisfy our real needs. Some of us have chronically held back on paying our bills and debts, even when we had the money to pay them. Or we have faithfully kept up our payments to one or two creditors and neglected the others. Some of us have simply ignored our debts for some time, hoping against hope that somehow they would miraculously get paid.

Some of us have been compulsive spenders, showering ourselves with things we neither need nor wanted. When we felt needy or lacking, we splurged on something we could not afford. We spent impulsively, incurred debt, felt guilty, promised never to do it again, and only repeated the same cycle the next time the feeling of "not enough" came up. Having overspent, we often had nothing to show for it and wondered where all that money went. Some compulsive spenders are not actually in debt, but they are still welcome in D.A. The only requirement for membership in Debtors Anonymous is a desire to avoid incurring unsecured debt.

Some of us have been compulsive paupers, leaving ourselves broke time and again, struggling from one financial crisis to the next. Then there are those of us who find it almost impossible to spend money on ourselves. The TV breaks and stays broken; that pair of shoes, ready for retirement, is made to work yet another year; and even medical and dental problems go unattended.

This disease affected our vision of ourselves and of the world around us. It led us to believe that we were "not enough"—at home, at work, in social situations, in love relationships. It also led us to believe that there is not enough out there in the world for us. The disease manufactured a sense of impoverishment in all that we did and saw.

In reaction to this, we withdrew into a dream world, fretted over money, and avoided responsibilities.

How Did Compulsive Debting Affect Our Lives?

The use of unsecured credit destroyed our self-esteem, hurt our families, and created an assortment of other problems. We were scared. We had sleepless nights. We dreaded opening the mailbox for fear of what we would find. We were hounded by endless computer statements, bill collectors, and lawyers. We may even have developed physical symptoms from worry. Family members or friends snubbed us, or more often we avoided them, because we owed them money. Others, who had sympathized with us at first, eventually got tired of hearing us complain of never having enough to make ends meet.

As we sat at our first D.A. meeting, we were hurting from many losses: loss of income, which had been eaten up by debt and compulsive spending; loss of faith; loss of self-respect and peace of mind; loss of friends; and sometimes loss of health, job, or family. Many of us had sought help from various individuals or organizations, only to come away feeling that nobody understood our problem. Our loneliness caused us to withdraw more and more into ourselves. We lost vitality and interest in life. Many of us actually became paralyzed from fear and discouragement. We could not work or take proper care of ourselves or our loved ones. Some of us thought we were going crazy, and others contemplated suicide.

This sense of despair, or "hitting bottom," was the first step in our recovery in Debtors Anonymous. We saw that our own attempts to scheme and manipulate our debts never worked. We admitted that we were powerless over debt. We were ready to ask for help.

Why Do We Join D.A.?

Most of us have been unwilling to admit we were compulsive debtors. No person likes to think he or she is different from his or her fellows. Therefore, it is not surprising that our adult lives have been characterized by countless vain attempts to prove we could handle our finances like other people. The idea that somehow, someday we will control our finances is the great obsession and fantasy of every compulsive debtor.

Debt, like alcohol for the alcoholic, food for the compulsive overeater and gambling for the compulsive gambler, is the false crutch that fed our fantasy and magnified our obsession. The persistence of the illusion is astonishing. Many pursue it to the gates of mental institutions, prison and suicide.

We learned that we had to concede fully to our innermost selves that we were compulsive debtors. This is the first step in our recovery. With reference to debt, the delusion that we are like other people, or presently may be, has to be smashed.

We have lost our ability to control our debt. We know that no compulsive debtor ever regains control. All of us felt at times that we were regaining control, but such intervals—usually brief— were inevitably followed by still less control, which led in time to pitiful and incomprehensible demoralization. We are convinced that debtors of our type are in the grip of a progressive illness. Over any considerable period of time we get worse, never better.

Therefore, in order to lead normal, happy and useful lives, we try to practice to the best of our ability certain principles in all our daily affairs.

How Does a Person Get Solvent through the D.A. Program?

He or she does this by first bringing about a progressive personality change within himself or herself. This is accomplished by having faith in—and trying to understand—the basic concepts of the Twelve Steps of Debtors Anonymous.

There are no shortcuts to gaining this *faith* and *understanding*. Recovery from one of the most baffling, insidious, compulsive addictions will require diligent effort. *Honesty* and *willingness* are the key words in our recovery.

Is Knowing Why We Got into Debt Important?

Not as a rule. Of the D.A. members who had psychiatric treatment, none have found a knowledge of why they used debt to be of value in stopping it.

What Are Some of the Factors that Might Cause a Person to Become a Compulsive Debtor?

Inability and Unwillingness to Accept Reality

Hence, the escape into the dream world of debt, pawning the future to avoid the responsibilities and challenges of the present.

Emotional Insecurity

Here, a compulsive debtor finds he or she is emotionally comfortable only when he or she has "enough" money or credit to do or get what he or she wants. It is not uncommon to hear a D.A. member say, "The only time I felt I really belonged was when I knew I could pick up the check. Then I felt secure and comfortable. I often knew I was destroying myself, but for the moment, I had a certain sense of security."

Immaturity

A desire to have all the good things in life without any great risk of rejection on his or her part seems to be the common character pattern of the problem debtor. Many D.A. members accept the fact that they were unwilling to grow up. Subconsciously they felt they could avoid mature responsibility for their affairs by borrowing or deferring payment for that which they felt they needed, and as the debts mounted the struggle to escape responsibility finally became a subconscious obsession.

Big Shotism

Also, a compulsive debtor seems to have a strong inner urge to be a "big shot" and needs to have the feeling of being all-powerful. The compulsive debtor is willing to do anything to maintain the image of himself or herself that he or she wants others to see, including business associates and immediate family.

Fear of Prosperity

Then, too, there is the theory that the compulsive debtor subconsciously fears the consequences of prosperity and uses debt to impoverish himself or herself. There is evidence among D.A. members to support this theory.

What Is the First Thing a Compulsive Debtor Ought to Do in Order to Recover?

The compulsive debtor needs to be willing to accept the fact that he or she is in the grip of a progressive illness, and he or she needs to have a desire to get well. Our experience has shown that the D.A. program will always work for any person who has a desire to stop using debt. However, it will seldom work for the man or woman who cannot, or will not, face squarely the facts about this illness.

How Can You Tell If You Are a Compulsive Debtor?

Only you can make that decision. Most people turn to D.A. when they become willing to admit that their debt has them licked. Also, in D.A. a compulsive debtor is described as a person whose debt has caused growing and continuing problems in any part of his or her life.

Many D.A. members went through humiliating and degrading experiences before they were ready to accept help. Others were faced with a slow, subtle deterioration which finally brought them to the point of admitting defeat.

Questionnaire

Most compulsive debtors will answer yes to at least eight of the following 15 questions.

	Yes	No
1. Are your debts making your home life unhappy?	___	___
2. Does the pressure of your debts distract you from your daily work?	___	___
3. Are your debts affecting your reputation?	___	___
4. Do your debts cause you to think less of yourself?	___	___
5. Have you ever given false information in order to obtain credit?	___	___
6. Have you ever made unrealistic promises to your creditors?	___	___

	Yes	No

7. Does the pressure of your debts make you careless of the welfare of your family? ___ ___

8. Do you ever fear that your employer, family or friends will learn the extent of your total indebtedness? ___ ___

9. When faced with a difficult financial situation, does the prospect of borrowing give you an *inordinate* feeling of relief? ___ ___

10. Does the pressure of your debts cause you to have difficulty in sleeping? ___ ___

11. Has the pressure of your debts ever caused you to consider getting drunk? ___ ___

12. Have you ever borrowed money without giving adequate consideration to the rate of interest you are required to pay? ___ ___

13. Do you usually expect a negative response when you are subject to a credit investigation? ___ ___

14. Have you ever developed a strict regimen for paying off your debts, only to break it under pressure? ___ ___

15. Do you justify your debts by telling yourself that you are superior to the "other" people, and when you get your "break" you'll be out of debt overnight? ___ ___

How did you score? If you answered yes to eight or more of these questions, the chances are that you have a problem with compulsive debt, or are well on your way to having one.

If this is the case, today can be a turning point in your life. We have all arrived at this crossroad. One road, a soft road, lures you on to further despair, illness, ruin, and in some cases, mental institutions, prison, or suicide. The other road, a more challenging road, leads to self-respect, solvency, healing, and personal fulfillment. We urge you to take the first difficult step onto the more solid road *now.*

A Brief History of Debtors Anonymous

Debtors Anonymous was begun in 1968 when a core group of recovering members from Alcoholics Anonymous held their first meeting to discuss the problems they were experiencing with money. They called themselves the "Penny Pinchers" and later "Capital Builders." The members of this group made daily deposits of their funds into savings accounts because they believed that their financial problems stemmed from an inability to save money. As days and months passed, the group's members began to understand that their monetary problems did not stem from an inability to save, but rather from the inability to become solvent. In early 1971, the essence of the D.A. program unfolded with the discovery and understanding that the act of debting itself was the threshold of this disease and that the only solution was to work the Twelve Steps of Alcoholics Anonymous.

After two years, the group of recovering A.A. members disbanded. Meetings came and went. D.A. was established permanently in 1976 when two or three people began meeting on Wednesday evenings in the Rectory of St. Stephen's Church in New York. Within the year, a second meeting was organized, and Debtors Anonymous was reborn. As of this printing, there are more than 500 registered, listed D.A. meetings in almost all fifty states and 21 countries around the world.

In 1987, the first General Service Conference of Debtors Anonymous was held in the auditorium of St. Vincent's Hospital in New York City. The conference was a truly wonderful event—but not at all like the conferences we know today. There were no hotels, no committee meeting rooms, no Debtor's Ball or talent show, and no funds to host the conference. But there were lots of camaraderie, a commitment to D.A. unity, and a Higher Power.

Since the first conference, D.A. has grown in numbers and the strength and quality of its members' recovery have continued to improve. Numerous literature pamphlets have been published, annual World Conferences have been held, the quarterly *Ways and Means* newsletter has been established, D.A. has accepted Business Debtors Anonymous (BDA) as a full partner, and the D.A. site on the World Wide Web (www.debtorsanonymous.org) has been launched.

The publication of this book, *A Currency of Hope*, culminates seven years of effort by the entire Fellowship and launches Debtors Anonymous into the 21st century as a truly global organization dedicated, as it has always been, to its primary purpose: helping the compulsive debtor who still suffers.

How to Find Debtors Anonymous

At the time of this printing, there are more than 500 known listed meetings of Debtors Anonymous in almost all fifty states of the United States. Known meetings also exist on five continents: North America, South America, Europe, Asia, and Australia, and in 21 countries.

The Debtors Anonymous General Service Board, Inc. maintains an office through which you can obtain additional information about D.A. worldwide. Please write to the following address for information:

D.A. General Service Office
P.O. Box 920888
Needham, MA 02492-0009
(781) 453-2743

In many larger metropolitan areas in the U.S., you may find a listing for a local Debtors Anonymous telephone number in the local telephone directory. Local social service agencies that make referrals to Twelve Step programs may also have information about Debtors Anonymous in their areas. Other traditional sources for locating Twelve Step meetings, such as newspapers, clergy, community service centers, and referral services, also may help you find D.A. meetings in your area.

Debtors Anonymous has a web site on the World Wide Web:

www.debtorsanonymous.org.

Information available through this web site includes general facts about D.A., information for the media, questions to ask yourself to determine if D.A. may be appropriate for you, information to access registered online groups, literature order forms, and current news for members.

Business Debtors Anonymous (BDA) gives information specific to business owners and self-employed professionals. BDA is fully embraced by Debtors Anonymous, but it has distinct concerns of special interest to its members.

On A Higher Power

Step Two of the Twelve Steps of Debtors Anonymous suggests that we come to believe in a power greater than ourselves that can restore us to sanity. Based on the long experience and traditions of all Twelve-Step fellowships, Debtors Anonymous has never attempted, nor would ever attempt, to define or limit what this Higher Power is or means. All members of the D.A. Fellowship have the absolute right to define this 'Higher Power' as they choose.

As the stories were being collected for inclusion in the book, the authors shared their experiences openly, giving of themselves so that others may recover from compulsive debting. When editing began on the book, the Debtors Anonymous General Service Board, Inc. faced an editing choice concerning the authors' references to the God of their understanding.

For continuity, one editing choice was to use the term "Higher Power" consistently throughout the book. This choice would have meant that the words used by the original author would have been changed. However, after careful consideration and with respect for the authors, it was decided that each story would remain in the author's own voice.

Therefore, in *A Currency of Hope*, each author has used his or her own term for the "God of our understanding." In addition, the terminology used in these stories is that of the individual author, and the opinions expressed are solely those of the people who wrote them. D.A. suggests that you take only what is helpful to you in your own spiritual journey and turn the rest over to a Higher Power of your own understanding.

With Gratitude and Appreciation
to Alcoholics Anonymous

In 1935 Bill W. and Dr. Bob founded Alcoholics Anonymous and gave birth to a spiritual foundation for recovery from alcoholism. Through their severe trials and inspirational efforts, they developed a proven method of recovery that works not only for alcoholism, but also for many serious addictions. Since then, they and their fellow members of A.A. have built a 'Road to Recovery' through the Twelve Steps and Twelve Traditions that has offered experience, strength, and hope to the untold millions of people who suffer from severe addictions.

We, the members of Debtors Anonymous, wish to thank Alcoholics Anonymous for opening the door to the joy of recovery and for proving—beyond any doubt—that the promises of the program do come true. We also appreciate A.A.'s generous permission to adapt the original Twelve Steps and Twelve Traditions to our program of recovery from the disease of compulsive debting.

Above all, we in D.A. wish to express our everlasting gratitude to a "God of our understanding" for the spiritual inspiration and strength in which all recovering addicts find our hope and our joy.

OUR STORIES

No Longer a Thief

This woman stopped taking from others after
learning how to give to herself.

Why was the police car in front of our house? Had something happened to Mom or Dad? I entered the house through the garage door; the front door was for holidays or guests.

Sitting around our kitchen table were my Mom and Dad, along with two police officers. I was told to sit at the table, this same table where I ate with the family, or played Scrabble, or poured drinks for Mom and Dad. Today the faces were all serious and angry—even disgusted. On the kitchen table were black-and-white drawings with the word "suspect" and the description: White female, five-foot-five, one hundred-twenty pounds, blonde, approximate age, twelve to fifteen years.

I was quiet that day. I listened intently as my parents explained why stealing is bad and wrong—even dangerous. My parents said they were ashamed of me, so disappointed. I looked in my Mom's eyes and saw hatred. I already thought she was jealous of me. More than once in her drunkenness, she had told me I was not pretty or smart. Often she said I would not get so much attention if people knew who I really was. And that day I knew she was right. I was so terrified that I never stole anything from that store again.

But a few months went by and I needed make-up. I used a lot of make-up, but had trouble choosing the right kind. I couldn't afford to make a mistake, so I just took it. If it was not perfect, it wouldn't hurt. I knew that if I could just have the right make-up, I would be good, beautiful, and lovable.

When I was younger, I had enjoyed frequent walks to the neighborhood Quick-Stop with my friends for candy or a popsicle, some very sweet treat. During those walks, I would reluctantly reveal that I had only a small amount of change, so my friends would pool their money to get me a treat too. I must be lovable I would think; friends buy me treats. My parents praised me to their friends for being careful with money. My sister, on the other hand, could not hold on to money: "Money burns a hole in that girl's pocket," my dad would often say.

At Christmas there were many sweets, presents, cards, visitors, calls, and festivities, but it was too much at once and only once a year. The time it took to unwrap everything was awesome! I would open one present after another, but it seemed as though I was looking for something that was never there. There was too much pressure to be surprised and happy about the gifts, and I knew I could never be grateful enough. I was embarrassed. I didn't let anyone know I felt this way, of course. I would be in a store soon, and there I would see something that would make the difference. I would take it; then I would be satisfied.

As I grew up, I became a sophisticated thief. I stole from friends and family, department stores, and small businesses. I was out of control. I had gotten everything I demanded, and still I felt empty. Perhaps more would make a difference the next time.

By the age of thirty, I had been married to the man of my childhood dreams for ten years. We had our second brand-new home in the suburbs, a nice new car in the two-car garage, and a new BMW touring motorcycle. We had a beautiful, healthy one-and-a-half-year-old son. Our family was complete now, yet I was miserable. I felt bad and ugly. I felt love only for my son and believed I had become completely unlovable. It took little more than two years to lose everything but the responsibility of caring for my son.

I had been clean and sober four years and had cleaned up much "wreckage from the past," as they say in A.A. Around the fellowship, I was known as a woman who took her sobriety seriously. I worked the Steps. I read and loved the Big Book of Alcoholics Anonymous. I kept regular contact with my sponsor and my sponsees. I was even in therapy. I was truly committed to doing my emotional work and my family of origin inventory. I wanted to be free, yet I was afraid most of the time. And no matter how hard I worked and budgeted, I never had enough money to get through the month.

I took in boarders, though I hated people living in the house with me and my son to meet expenses. I used my two credit cards at the end of every month for a treat for us or gifts for someone. I would try to do without all month, then I would need relief. Credit cards or stealing seemed the only way. I didn't plan to steal; it was usually an afterthought. I knew something was very wrong that I felt so bad and was still stealing. I was particularly vulnerable at the cosmetic counter.

I was willing to pay for mascara, but not the two lip liners. What was happening to me? I had never been caught stealing. My only close call was that day long ago in the kitchen with the police officers.

Early one fall, I was out with a friend. In the middle of my whining about money problems, my friend said she was not at all sure my problem was debting or compulsive spending. She did tell me that she had been going to a program called Debtors Anonymous and that this program was helping her to live free of worry about money. I trusted this friend and, on that alone, I went to my first D.A. meeting. I hated being new. I hated being there at all. It felt so shameful! I did not even understand the word "debting," although I did feel some understanding of compulsive spending. I was sure my problem was that I wanted too much: I needed help to control my spending so I could have enough money to pay all my bills every month, including those awful credit card balances that continued to grow in spite of my paying the minimum every month. I couldn't see how to do it without credit cards.

I did cut up my credit cards during the first month of going to D.A. meetings. I was terrified. I suffered from sleeplessness, panic attacks, and rage. I used my small prudent reserve in a few months trying to do it all without credit cards or boarders. I would pay all my bills, including credit card debts and my student loans. Then I would see there was not enough money left for us to live on for the rest of the month. I tried to juggle the amount I spent on food or gas, and I cut out all entertainment for me or my son. The deprivation would make me crazy each month. My life was getting worse: It was harder and now, I began to bounce checks at the end of the month.

Out of desperation, I finally began to talk in meetings, sharing my confusion, anger and terror. I began to have Pressure Relief Groups and after about nine months, surrendered to the truth that I really could not meet my needs and continue to make debt repayment. I was horrified at the thought of inviting bill collectors into my already terrifying life, but I saw I had no choice. I had seen others in the fellowship learn to place their own needs first, and their lives were changing. They were less worried. These people were talking about taking vacations and having fun. I wanted to stop stealing. I too wanted to be free.

I worked hard at my D.A. recovery. I loved and used all the tools available to me. I attended meetings and talked to people on the phone, sometimes bookending a shopping trip. I even made phone calls from stores when I felt that dizzy confusion. I prayed a lot to my God for direction and guidance. This new way of living required such focus. I fielded the phone calls from bill collectors. I cried and screamed my way through the shame and the humiliation. I finally began to separate myself from what I earn, own, or owe, but I was still overwhelmed by the feeling that there was really not enough for me in the world. Whenever I did begin to believe there might be enough, I would shrink with the feeling that I was not enough. Then I would steal and hate myself even more. I dared to talk about stealing in meetings. I had felt so alone with my shame.

After a year and a half in D.A., my world filled with death and grief. Within a summer, twelve people I knew and cared about died or were murdered. I hurt, crying for weeks. I rarely left my house, only occasionally going to my favorite meetings where I would just sit and cry. Sometimes I shared and people just listened. Thank God no one tried to fix me or asked me to leave. One afternoon, I came back from a meeting feeling quiet, not so sad. I went to a store to buy a few things I needed, and I saw a large assortment of flowers outside the store. I took two plants and put them in the back of my car. I drove home and carefully hung my beautiful new plants from the deck. For weeks, I spent most of my daylight hours sitting on the deck either crying, reading fairy tales, or staring quietly into space. I needed the flowers for hope and for their beauty.

I sat on the deck and looked at my flowers and suddenly understood, for the first time in my life, that I stole because I believed there was not enough in this world for me and that I did not deserve anything good or beautiful. I believed that I was bad, ugly, even rotten to the core, as I had heard my mother say so often when I was a little girl. I believed I was unlovable. In that moment, I understood that every time I stole I was reinforcing those beliefs I had picked up in my childhood. I cried and through my tears, I asked God to be interested in me, my life, and to help me to believe that I was good, beautiful, and lovable. I needed to open myself up to the generosity of God.

There were many more months of tears that year, but I never felt alone again. I never stole anything, even when I had intense feelings of lack or deprivation. Now I was on different footing. I was learning to care for myself and be the grown-up in my own life.

Five more years have passed since then. I stay close to D.A. I truly love my group and have stayed in service to my Monday night meeting. I continue to use the tools of the program, and I love the action plans that are generated from my Pressure Relief Groups. My action steps now consist of shopping for new furniture and saving for a trip to Europe with my teenage son. I receive loving encouragement to be gentle and loving to myself. I am supported by D.A. to give myself love, comfort, even luxury. I have come a long way on this journey. Stealing is something I used to do. Now I can trust myself and my God to love and take care of me.

In a visions meeting in my second year of recovery in D.A., I saw myself holding hands with a partner. I had a feeling of love, warmth, and comfort. Today I have that partnership with myself. I am no longer consumed by the isolation or the tragic loneliness that a compulsive, addicted person knows. My family is in my life again. What a miracle! Now I love and care about them just the way they are. Today, the greatest gifts from my recovery work are the relationships I have with myself and others. It has happened: I am good, beautiful, and lovable! Thanks D.A.! And thank God for the Twelve Steps.

I've Come A Long Way, Honey

An indulged child learned how to get money for what she wanted,
but it took jail and D.A. for her to learn how to earn the money.

I remember that the first time I told my story was at the ripe old age of fourteen. I was going to Alateen meetings, because my Dad was an alcoholic. A little ol' lady "blue hair" Bible study group had asked a teenager to speak on "growing up in an alcoholic home." I was asked to speak. My opening sentence was, "Have you ever lived in Hell"? I don't know where that remark came from.

Today, I believe God was speaking through me. I remember that my audience did not understand that alcoholism was a disease. I know now that I didn't get it either. That is why it was so hard for me to grasp the concept that my money issues are a disease I have no control over.

Being born into an affluent family was not a gift for me. I was raised with a maid to clean my room, make my bed, etc., which I later recognized as detrimental to my growth. Having been raised that way, I have always had a feeling of entitlement, "one up," "better than," and many other grandiose ideas.

I began stealing money from my father's billfold when I was six. While Dad was drunk every night watching TV, I would slip in my parents' bedroom, take $5 or $10, and go to the little neighborhood grocery. I would buy candy to treat the neighborhood. I always was buying things for people. I never felt they liked me, so I bought them things thinking then maybe they would like me.

I remember having a charge account at this little grocery. Sometimes I would want more candy than I had money for, so I charged it. Of course, my parents had charge accounts all over town. My need to buy people was increased by a weight problem that had begun when I was three years old.

I learned at an early age to do one of two things. I might go to a store, buy what I wanted, and charge it. Then I'd watch the mail for the bill and throw it away. Next month the statement would show a balance due, and my Dad would most likely think he had just forgotten. My other way was to charge whatever I wanted, and listen to them scream, knowing it would blow over.

When I went away to college, my Dad opened a checking account for me, depositing an amount on the first of the month. I was to pay for dorm rent and food and to write a check for anything else I needed. It did not take me long to discover I could write checks with no regard to my checkbook balance and get a written lecture when the bank statement came directly to my Dad's office. He would write me a letter, listing each check with an explanation on why I should not spend the money.

I grew up knowing that my Mother wrote "hot checks" all the time. My Dad would frequently come home ranting and raving when the bank called about her bounced checks. For some reason, it was expected because wives were considered "dumb" and "incompetent." My mother also taught me it was okay to charge something, hide it under the bed, and then lie that it wasn't new. Another message from my Mother was that God will answer your prayers when you're good enough, but no one will ever want to marry you.

The stage had been set, and believe me, the actress in my story played it to the hilt. The first man that came along wanting to marry me proved her wrong, and I married him even though I couldn't stand him. All my friends had big diamonds and many wedding parties. Not to be outdone, and certainly not one to make my family look bad, I married him. A $10,000 wedding and reception in the Sixties was a major blowout. Ninety days later we were separated and our divorce had been filed.

I moved to Dallas intending to be a big girl and support myself. The only problem was no one had ever taught me how. I certainly did not know how to get a job, balance a checkbook, or live on what I made. The truth of the matter was that I was a sick, spoiled brat. My grandparents lived in Dallas, and I could get anything from them: money, food, clothes, and love. My grandfather wanted to buy me a car, but my father said, "No, she made her bed—let her lie in it."

I quickly found husband Number Two. He was a nice, good-looking engineer with a new car, money in the bank, credit cards, and stock. I drained him before we even got married and again after. Shortly after we married, he was laid off from his job. At this time, I was pregnant. We had a new car and many bills.

Those were real crazy years when I charged every credit card to the max, and then some. When the bills came in, I threw them away or hid them. I thought somehow money would magically appear, and then I would pay them. I would lie to bill collectors on the phone. It was crazy-making.

Still, out of all of this I had a wonderful, warm, intelligent son for whom I thank God every day of my life. My husband and I divorced, and then I had to raise and support my son alone. It would be lying to say I did either one very well; I didn't. I worked for a while, but I was caught stealing a lot of money. It still amazes me that they did not file charges against me. I would take my son to day care and then play all day. After I lost that job, I would visit friends, shop, or do whatever I felt like. I never paid my child care bills and didn't look for another job. I was living a lie.

Shortly after, I discovered the wonderful world of borrowing. Now my working days were really over. I was able to borrow almost any amount of money, so I borrowed large sums. I never borrowed intending not to pay it back. I told the truth as I saw it each time I borrowed. I truly do not know how I thought I would pay the money back. I lived in a fairyland of grandiosity.

For the next four years, I was in a relationship, supporting five people. I began to be arrested for writing hot checks. When the sheriff's department would come to pick me up, I would call the judge at home. That worked for a while, but it ended. I retained a good attorney capable of getting the charges dropped. This happened a dozen times or more.

My attorney had finally said, "I'm not doing you any favors anymore." One day I was picked up on another hot check charge and bond was set at $10,000. At a pre-trial hearing the District Attorney's office supervisor told me they had quit counting when I reached the $100,000 mark. Another attorney negotiated probation for me. I've heard that probation is nothing more than a slow walk to the penitentiary. For me, it was rapid.

So, off to county jail I went for six months. I cried for twenty hours a day and was a big pain to everyone. I broke all the rules, but I did start accepting reality. My old attorney and my father discussed getting me out, but I realized it was obvious I needed to go to the "Big House" or my pattern would never be broken.

I was sentenced to six years but was paroled after eighteen months, because political strings were pulled. My parents bought me a car and a new wardrobe, and I went to work. My criteria for a job was only that I wanted to work as many hours as possible and not work with any women. After coming home, I did pretty well and kept my nose clean. Later on was when my real recovery began. I found Adult Children of Alcoholics (ACOA), and for the first time in my life, I began to feel normal.

I started a cleaning business, never thinking how I would pay my employees, or buy supplies and equipment with no money. I had clients, but it was a constant struggle. I started praying about it, and shortly my clients were asking me if I could do this...or that. I certainly never said no, so in a very short time, I found myself in a remodeling business that I knew nothing about. But, I knew how to con my way in, get the job, and find people to do it.

However, I needed a lot more knowledge than I had—two contractors took me for about $13,000. For about three weeks I robbed Peter to pay Paul. Paul dropped dead and Peter left town. In just three weeks I had written $6,000 worth of hot checks for the business. I had once again crossed that line and written hot checks.

I had heard of Debtors Anonymous and had even recorded my spending for a time. Now it was time to face that although ACOA had helped me tremendously, the bottom line was that my core issues were money and food. When I walked into my first meeting, I felt so much shame. I was devastated. I prayed that I would not see anyone I knew, but there were some familiar faces.

I will never forget my first meeting. Someone said they had not written a hot check that week, and I almost fell out of my chair. I did not say a word that night except to say my name, almost making one up. When the meeting was over, I waited outside for everyone to leave. When almost everyone was gone, I went back in and told the chairperson who I was and that I had been in the penitentiary for hot checks, and that I currently had $6,000 in bad checks out.

Pressure Relief Meetings had been mentioned in the meeting, and I understood what they were. I said I thought I needed a Pressure Relief Meeting immediately. This person looked at me and said, "Yes, I think you need one." The next Monday night after the D.A. meeting I went prepared for the Pressure Relief Meeting, but scared out of my wits. I felt so much shame that I can't put those feelings into words. My Pressure Relief Group (PRG) advised me to borrow money to cover the checks, but I did nothing. I went back to my magical thinking that money would fall from the heavens, my old grandiosity, and the feeling that I was above the law.

The PRG team told me I needed to contact everyone I had written checks to asking for a thirty-day reprieve. This I did, and my creditors all agreed. I also followed up with a letter. That would give me the needed time to borrow the money and pay off the checks. Beyond phone calls and letters, I did nothing to create the money. Remember, I believed that money was going to fall from the sky or that someone would mail me what I needed. But I kept going to meetings, writing my money down, and turning it over.

One day, someone from the sheriff's department rang my doorbell with a warrant for my arrest. I wasn't home. I did not have a fear of going back to the penitentiary, really, but I had an extreme fear of going to jail. For the next four days, I did not work. I was so frozen with fear that I went only to meetings and talked to people. Then a miraculous thing happened in my life.

Someone had given me the Third Step prayer. It was on a card, and I stuck it in one of the air conditioning vents in my car. I said that prayer all day, every day. With all my heart, I believe this was the beginning for me.

On awakening the fifth morning after the warrant was issued, my attorney's name, face, and energy was all around me. I knew God had answered my prayers. I called the attorney and told him the truth. He suggested I pay the one check that could result in a felony charge.

I had $400 but needed $600 more. Someone in D.A. had the $600, and through meditation, journaling and daily reading made the decision to loan the money to someone who needed it. I put up collateral to secure the loan, paid off the check, and the case was dropped. I paid back the loan at $50 a week

I still had $5,000 in misdemeanor checks out. Did I take care of those? No, I went back into that magical thinking, went back to work, went to meetings and talked to my sponsor. I said the Third Step prayer.

I was stopped downtown for a traffic violation in the spring of the following year. The officer did not have time to wait for a sheriff to come pick me up, so he told me to go take care of my personal business, knowing there were five misdemeanor warrants for my arrest. At this point, I started to believe in God. Up to this point, I was skeptical about God, but this one was larger than I was in the miracle department. Miraculously, all of those checks were taken care of with God's help.

I continued to write my numbers down, go to meetings, call my sponsor, talk to God, say the Third Step prayer, and work. After about six months of driving for a courier company, my spirit started to come back. I was regaining me! My confidence was building, maybe slowly, but it was building. The fun, creative side of me had been dead for so long that I had worried it would never come back. Lo and behold, one day while driving, I started to think about what I could do if I were in the courier business for myself. I decided to go on my own on my one-year anniversary with the present company. With twelve clients, I was in business for myself.

Today, at times, I still do not believe I am liked, intelligent, competent, trustworthy, or loving. After a while, boredom and my creative side of me started working again. I started entertaining ideas of a large woman- and minority-owned courier company. With all of that, I could not go wrong. I began telling my sponsor about it. I had a strong belief that if it was God's will, then it would happen. I do not believe I ever felt so strongly before. I plodded along doing the footwork, and eventually, someone offered to invest in my company. That's when the real work began. The whole thing is a God deal, and it continues to be.

The company has had its share of problems. I know it will not come as a surprise that most of them have centered around my cash flow or lack of it. I projected about $75,000 short, but by turning it over, sometimes on a minute-by-minute basis, we will survive. I always have to remember that this is God's corporation, not mine. So many miracles!

In the last six years I had become estranged from most of my family. But lately, that is starting to heal. Another miracle!

I continue to read daily meditation books, write my numbers down, turn my will and my life over to God, call my sponsor, thank God, go to meetings and do service work. If it were not for the grace of God, countless close friends, and D.A., I would be not be here today.

The World's Best Credit Card Marketer

This man pitched credit cards until he sold himself on them.
He found relief in the D.A. principles.

When I sat down at my first Debtors Anonymous meeting seven years ago, I had no experience and little knowledge of the Twelve Steps. I just knew I was in a lot of pain, and I wanted it to stop.

The meeting focused on tools of D.A., and the tool that day was "awareness." When I heard them define the term, I knew that, uncomfortable as I felt, I had to talk. I waited until near the end of the meeting before I held up my hand and began. "My name is _____," I said, "and I'm not sure what to call myself. But for the past four years I was a credit card marketer." There was a moment of silence; then each group member reacted in their own way. Several just stared, and one man made the sign of the cross, but most just laughed at the irony. Their laughter let me know they welcomed me. My recovery had begun.

Until 1985, I didn't even know how a credit card worked. Oh, I knew that you used it at the store and had to pay it off later on, but I knew nothing about the concept of revolving credit. I worked in the registration office of a university in New York City, working my way through graduate school. Many people paid their tuition with credit cards, and very often someone would say, "What do you mean, declined? Why? I just sent in a payment. I'm below my limit!" I hadn't the faintest notion of what they were talking about, so I'd just go along and say "Well, sir, they don't tell us why. Maybe the payment hasn't gotten there yet." Usually they'd pull out another card and charge the fees to it.

At that time I carried only one card, which required that it be paid off each month. I always did, although that frequently left me without enough to make it until my next paycheck. The idea of not buying anything you didn't have cash for at the moment never occurred to me. Then I finally got my first revolving credit card, and my descent into insanity began. "This is pretty cool," I thought. "I'll charge something and take a couple of months to pay it off. Boy, that's easy."

Sure. And if you look hard enough, you can see the edge of the world, because it's flat.

When I finished graduate school, I was involved in a relationship. When my girlfriend complained that I should be making more money, with a graduate degree and all, I ignored the fact that she was doing nothing to bring in more income herself. I dutifully went down to an employment agency, completely changing my personal appearance and ignoring the inner voice that told me that I really should be moving back to Texas. I did the "adult" thing and tried to find a respectable job.

I was actually hired by the first firm I interviewed with, as a secretary in the Travel Department of one of New York City's major banks. Seven months later I transferred to a writing position in the credit card division. By this time, I still had only one credit card and was starting to worry because the balance on it was about $400, and I was paying only the minimum while the balance went steadily up each month. But instead of paying it off, I used the card to buy several suits for my new position. Of course I searched around for bargains, buying only at the lowest price. Who can estimate the eventual price of each use, with the interest added on?

At about this same time the banks began experimenting with a new type of product called the "affinity" credit card. These cards were marketed to people who were members of certain organizations or loyal to causes, with the promise that a percentage of each charge would go to the beloved organization. My employer happened to be marketing a card for the alumni of my graduate school, and when the project director asked me to accept the card and report on how quick the response time for each step was, I happily agreed. By this time I already had a vague sense that my credit card behavior wasn't too smart, so I said to myself, "I just won't use this card; I'm taking it only as an experiment, and I won't ever use it." And I promptly put it into my wallet. It probably took a year before it was maxed out.

A year or two later came one of the surest signs that I was on my way to financial security: I crossed the threshold to the magic Kingdom of Gold. As soon as I was making enough money to qualify for my employer's Gold credit card, I shot my application in. And once again I uttered those wonderful words: "This time, with this card, I'll do it right. I won't let any charges revolve more than a month." In less than two years I had reached the $5,000 maximum.

In the meantime, what did my job find me doing each day? I would arrive at work, sit down at my desk, and try to figure out how to sell credit cards to people and how to get them to spend more and revolve more. When I tell my story at D.A. meetings, I always joke that I must have been very good at what I did, because it sure worked on me.

As part of the credit card marketing department, I wrote the "newsletters" inserted into the cardmembers' statements each month. I wrote articles featuring different vendors who were willing to sell unique items by telephone, using credit cards. The newsletter also featured fabricated correspondence asking about such items as credit card security, to which we could respond by describing one of the "services" we offered—for a modest fee, of course. Once a week we would have a departmental meeting, and the subject of these meetings was how to get our customers to spend more and revolve more. We introduced credit line increases, telling the customers we were doing this because they were "valued" and "responsible." We invented checks that looked just like your personal ones, but instead drew against your credit limit. You name it, and we did it. Anything for a dollar.

Another part of the job was analyzing which potential customers who applied were likely to be high chargers, and which ones were potential "charge-offs"—meaning that they might someday just say "I'm sorry, I can't pay any more." I wonder how the members of D.A. might have looked on their computer programs.

After two and a half years at this job, I accepted a position at another bank that offered a higher salary. Not that the salary would have made any difference in my standard of living. In less than four years, my salary had gone from $17,000 to $46,000, but my life grew increasingly more difficult each year. I was living in a dingy basement apartment. My self-esteem was so low that I didn't even own a bed; instead, I slept for five years on a second-hand couch. My money went in a hundred directions, most of which I cannot even remember today. At one point I decided to buy a plane ticket to San Francisco on the card that had to be paid off monthly, thinking that now I would have to pay the bill when it came in. Of course when it came due, I didn't have the money in my account, and after several calls from the company, I ended up charging it to one of my revolving cards.

It was about this same time that my credit began to be rejected at stores, meaning I was over the 10% "cushion" above the credit limit most banks provided. Most times I slipped through, but when I didn't, it was terribly humiliating. I also began bouncing checks, so I signed up for the overdraft protection on my checking account. Although I tried to keep a running total in my checkbook, when my statement came each month, I put it into a drawer unopened. My checking and even my savings accounts were always empty by the time my next paycheck came around, and I remember desperately calling the automated information line, trying to find out which checks had cleared, terrified that I had withdrawn too much cash and that my paycheck would not come before the paper started to bounce.

I also remember racing around the streets of Manhattan, trying to get cash advances on my credit cards so that I could continue to show the world a picture of myself as a man with money. Then, suddenly, things began to change. In October 1990, I sat in a Greenwich Village eatery, staring out at the dark, rainy, cold street. I have to get out of New York, I thought, but I don't have the money to do it. Outside of a 401K account, I had no money at all.

Less than 12 hours later, when I arrived at work the next morning, my boss told me she didn't think my job was right for me, or that I was right for it. She asked me if I would be willing to take three months' salary as severance pay. My mind racing quickly, I realized that she was talking about $10,000 to $12,000. Yes, I said. In November of that year, I left New York City and headed back to Texas. It was the first time I began to think that maybe there is a God.

Now that I'm home, I told myself, I'll put that horrible life behind me. I'll stop using my credit cards. And I promptly bounced my first rent check, telling myself that the balance on an ATM meant that cash was available to me, even if there were checks still outstanding. In my terror and shame, I drove through a red light, and it is only by the grace of God that the other drivers and I avoided each other.

In mid-January of 1991, I was browsing in a bookstore when I saw a book about getting out of debt. I drove to the public library and borrowed a copy. I started reading but shut it when it told me to cut up my credit cards. Although I had decided to use them no more, the thought of cutting them up hit me like a sledge hammer in the middle of my chest. So instead, I put them in an envelope, sealed it up, and hid them on my closet shelf. Late in January I was talking to a friend on the phone, and she was describing her own credit card problems. I told her about the book's advice, and she said, "Do you want to do it?" Gulp. "You mean right now?" "Sure," she replied. I got my scissors, fetched the cards, and cut them up. I felt a tremendous surge of relief and freedom.

Telling me to cut up my cards was not the only wonderful piece of advice that book offered. It also mentioned a group called Debtors Anonymous just for people like me. When I read about this group, I decided to go.

That night I was called out of town for several months, but I kept the book (The library later waived the large overdue fee because it was an emergency—my first D.A. miracle). And so in April 1991, I found myself sitting in a room confessing that I used to be on the other side. From that moment, I began to attend three meetings a week.

It took a while for the program to catch on with me. For six months I continued to pay on my credit cards by debting out of what was left of my 401K. It took me that long to find the courage to ask for a Pressure Relief Meeting, and my Pressure Relief Group promptly instructed me to stop payments, showing me that I could not afford to continue. That was when I finally admitted my powerlessness over debting. I wrote my creditors, explaining that I could not currently make payments and would pay when I became able to. It was at that point that I began to live for myself.

For several months I received calls, sometimes six daily, from the collections departments of the banks. Then they turned the accounts over to collectors, who called regularly, sometimes trying to shame me into paying money I didn't have. One called ten times in as many minutes and left an abusive message on my answering machine. I wrote to the company, threatening a complaint to the State Attorney General. Anger does wonders for self-esteem.

In the meantime, D.A. began to work miracles for me. Since I moved back to Texas, I had begun to nurture myself by returning to writing and photography, two of my passions. One night I was trying to look at some of my photographs, but the light in my apartment was too low. I picked up the book about how to get out of debt, and it opened to the passage where the author was urged by his friends (Pressure Relief Group) to buy a table he needed, even though he had bills coming in but no anticipated income. He bought the table, and unexpected money came in. So I went out that night and bought a lamp that flooded my apartment with light, believing that if I spent the extra money, it would be returned to me. My photographs never looked better. The next day, I got a call asking me to participate in an asthma medication study. Not only would the clinic buy my expensive medicine, it would pay me handsomely.

When my camera was stolen, an offer came several days later from one of my old bank bosses to do some freelance writing work The payment was almost exactly the cost of a new camera. Two months later, when the money came, I bought a new camera outfit. That very day, before I had unpacked it, I received a call saying the stolen one had been recovered with nothing missing. I returned the new camera to the store and tore up the check.

When I needed a new job, I tried to decide what kind of work I wanted. I settled on a bookstore and drove directly to the one closest to me. They had a sign up reading "Help Wanted." I applied and was hired four days later. Miracles all.

Today I find that I have enough to meet my needs. Money often comes to me mysteriously, in ways I could not have predicted. When my miracle bookstore job turned difficult, I prayed for God to give me guidance, to show me a sign that all was okay. Ten minutes later I found a $50 bill hidden in a book; two weeks later I found $96 folded in another.

Today, I still have debts amounting to almost $10,000, but I know that I will pay them off in time. By working the tools of D.A., calling my friends and sponsor, adhering to my spending plan, listening to my Pressure Relief Group and meticulously keeping records, the fear and shame about my debts have been removed. When I receive an occasional call from a creditor, my heart doesn't pound as it did even a year ago.

The greatest miracle in my life today is realizing that money is a small part of abundance. I don't have a lot of money, but I have mountains of abundance. I have myself, and I have a relationship with a loving God. Anything else dwindles in importance.

Loving As Money; Money As Love

Money became her measure for love, and finally her lover. In D.A. she learned to be present as a business woman, mother and wife.

I became obsessed with money when I was in the fourth grade. I asked my grandmother for "just a little" so I could go downtown to buy myself "a little something." It was as much my quick fix then as it became for me later as an adult.

Money in my pocket gave me something to do so I didn't have to see my loneliness, sit with it, or remain alone with it. Buying something gave me somewhere important to go, and with a rush of adrenaline and a feeling of excitement, I became worthwhile (for a little while) as I purchased my gift for the day. When I was given money, I was loved, simple as that. And knowing I could somehow always "get it" gave me a feeling of power and superiority that just turned out to be other words for egocentricity. It never made me feel good for very long. Then, I'd ask for more money. I didn't get what I needed. Instead of getting love, I only got a feeling of control and my ability to "act out."

As a teen looking good meant being wanted and admired. I was voted Best Dressed of the Senior Class. The school photographer took a picture of me all dressed up looking in the mirror at myself. The reflection of those sad baby-blue eyes and a ghost of a smile pasted on my face always reminded me of that Peggy Lee song, "Is That All There Is?"

I got married the summer after graduation, depressed and desperately lonely, and loving his large close-knit family and wanting company. I knew he'd be a good father and a hard worker, and he'd help me belong and fit in. And yes, look good.

We bought several homes and each time, I would start a major home improvement plan. I'd already changed complete living room furnishings several times. I would tire of them after several months and call the store, finding something wrong with them so they'd take them back. I always used credit, so I mostly got my way. Meanwhile, I wasn't very available to my children, not having much time for them, so driven I was by things. I was in love with those things.

I really believed that if my home looked good enough, people would want me. I wouldn't be alone.

After five homes, including lots of moving and marriage problems, my husband and I decided to start our own house-building business. I had a hard time staying in our home office handling customer calls, because we were bringing in a lot of money, and I wanted to spend it. We usually received one-half of the down payment for the homes up front. I saw it as mine and spendable. I talked our landholder into releasing part of our business property acreage to build a model home on. Then, the bank didn't require any down payment and gave us a full construction loan. I felt very clever and smug about pulling this off. I had no idea how we'd pay for that mortgage.

Soon it was clear my marriage was breaking up. I hardly had time for intimacy because I was so preoccupied with money. Somehow I had married a man who left me alone a lot, and money became my lover.

When I finally got the courage to look at our financial state and my marriage state. I decided to go, leaving it all for him. I figured he hadn't loved or wanted me, so he could have the bills. He soon had to file for bankruptcy, and our new model house was repossessed. I was on my way to another marriage, so it didn't take long for the old marriage to be a complete disaster. We simply moved, and ran up bills, and moved again. Finally we divorced, and I found myself in a little studio apartment. My children lived with their father. I had a table, rocker, and a mattress on the floor I bought for two dollars at a garage sale. I had trouble staying at any one job. I would get tired and hopeless, just barely surviving and living like a pauper. Usually I picked jobs that were unhealthy for me, acting out or getting fired. I thought they too owed me, and when they tired of my taking time off, rearranging my work schedule, or just playing, the job would end.

I finally landed a job where I was able to perform and earned a pretty good salary. I became fairly stable. I met my husband-to-be and moved to suburbia in an affluent area of town. He had a nice home, but it needed attention. Once again, without even seeing it, I went on a rampage of decorating and shopping and spending. But this time, because I was married to a man with a stable job and excellent credit history, I had credit cards! I can still remember how I felt when one of the salespeople at a department store called me by name after she rang up a sale, saying "Thank you, Mrs. _____."

I felt such a rush of importance and respect. I was finally fitting in with the rest of the community. I had buying power! I had a lovely home, my children were now with me, and I had a job where I was considered "the hub of the wheel," and a good salary: quite a respectable life. I felt so loved and admired.

After we financed our home a second time, using all our equity to pay off credit cards, we just spent up to our credit limit. Once again, I knew I was in trouble.

I started lying about my income. I acquired four major credit cards with high limits. Now I became really depressed. I was actually afraid to leave the house to go to work, because I'd been away from work for so long. I felt more and more isolated, more and more alone. I didn't want to see friends, because I couldn't look good anymore, and because even I didn't believe my big plans and schemes. My self-will and brainstorming for all these months had not worked, and now I was so afraid that I couldn't even think. Several months before coming to Debtors Anonymous, I realized I was doing some very sick and wrong things, and I had the feeling something was coming to an end. I thought it might be my life.

First, I took money from an investment account of my daughter's that was paid her from an accident settlement as a result of a drunken driver. Four hundred dollars had not yet been invested, and without her permission I asked for the check to be sent to me. I did not tell her, but just kept thinking and hoping I'd replace it. Finally, when school was about to begin, I charged her school clothes. I told her that instead of her using her money, I would deduct her clothes from what I owed her. It became so complicated that I finally broke down one afternoon and told her what I had really done and how bad I felt, mostly about how it felt to need money from my twelve-year-old daughter.

Next were the sad instances of the gift certificates. I charged certificates at two different department stores, for $50 each, in my daughter's name. I asked them if she get could get the cash back, if she didn't find anything, and the answer was yes. When I took my daughter with me to get the money, both stores made a big stink, saying she'd have to purchase something. We bought socks, and they refunded us the rest. All this for $90 cash and more debting. Worse, I was role modeling for my daughter how to charge, how to debt, and how to do something dishonest. Lucky her, for being the one to sign the certificates.

When I got to Debtors Anonymous, it was a Tuesday night in August 1992, the worst night of my life, I thought. I didn't say a word, hardly looking at anyone. I have never felt so shameful and so afraid. If I had tried to talk, I knew I would cry. I cried afterward all the way home. I did hear the suggestion of eight meetings in the next six weeks and to keep coming back. I did, too, attending two meetings a week, consistently. I took to heart the idea of keeping a spending record, and I did for the next two months. By the third meeting, I had accepted a new half-time position in a good place, with good folks. By the grace of God, it was just in time for me. By the fourth meeting, my husband came along. I heard him say he was afraid that things had gotten so bad that our relationship might not survive and that he hoped these meetings would "help me." I was amazed he had even spoken to a roomful of strangers, especially about our troubled marriage. I was really frightened, and it hit me that we were in deep trouble.

Then the weekend came, and all our kids were home. I got up early and went shopping. Hours later, I found myself in the dressing room at a department store shaking and sweating, thinking that I could not get out of this place and that I might have to have the saleswoman call my husband. I felt immobilized, unable to make a decision. I thought about how much I was missing at home, how this would have been a good time to talk to my son, and how I had wanted to see all of them, but now the day was half over. I finally got to my car and drove home, leaving my packages in the car to sneak in later. I had gone to the grocery store before I got home so I could say I was grocery shopping and doing "a few errands," my line for lying about shopping. Kinda like having "just a few drinks."

When I got home I felt sick and went to bed, where I cried so hard and long that I finally called for help. I called someone in the program. Luckily, he was calm and accepting, saying it sounded like I had gone out to try one last time and gotten the shakes, so I probably had reached bottom and really scared myself. He suggested that I pray and read Step One. I never thought I would be totally reliant on Step One, but now I was willing to do anything. I knew I was powerless over my spending and debting, and that only a Power greater than myself could help me now. Somehow I had believed my friend who had to get to Step One in order to stop drinking, but I didn't think I would ever be so out of control with my "silly ol' spending." That afternoon I made the decision to turn my life and my will over to the care of God. And I got out of bed!

Within two weeks my husband and I had our first Pressure Relief Group. Things looked bleak and hopeless, and I thought there were probably no choices. But for the first time, everything was down on paper, and reality was pretty clear. We listed a homework and action plan and scheduled our new Pressure Relief Group. It appeared we all felt better. I made my ideal wish list spending plan, writing down all my expenditures. I loved that part. Then I wrote my dream salary. Of course when I added it all up, I had overspent by $22,000. Even with an income of $100,000 a year, I was still short. Finally the disease had begun to speak to me!

Our next Pressure Relief Group was with the married couple, both in our program. My husband was skeptical, believing this program was great for my spending problem, but he didn't see why *he* needed it. He was concerned only with paying bills, that was all. The issue of trust arose, and I realized the reason we had separate checking accounts might have something to do with trust and secrets.

I was thankful for both of them taking responsibility for their joint debting, spending and pauper problems. Obviously this was not about just one person.

I learned about my spending and how when I felt deprived, or when my basic needs came last, after bill paying, I became compulsive and angry. I came to realize that looking good to hide feeling bad had never worked. It had never made me okay with myself, or lovable. I found that in my "terminal vagueness," I hadn't even known what my own business really made, though it was my business earnings that qualified us for a low-interest home loan, saving us money on our mortgage and greatly reducing our debt load.

In early December we went to an all-cash spending plan. Our best gift was a Christmas without credit. The day after Christmas, we looked at each other and smiled, knowing we owed no one anything and with the peace of mind that this was the right road now.

I had hoped we could be one of those program couples who could make a new life, forgive, and build new trust with our commitment to the program. But this is a dangerous, rampant, insidious disease that can kill, and sometimes there is too much damage and denial until it's too late.

Miracles happen. And this program works. It may not work the way we planned it or dreamed it, but the folks in the meetings and Pressure Relief Groups are messengers in the spirit of this life-saving and life-changing program. Now I have support and friendship, love and intimacy, and a new family in this program. I can now make proactive choices for growth and happiness for myself and my daughter, moving ahead to how I want to live my life. Today, instead of pretending and looking good to fit in so my family will love me, I am living openly, according to my true nature. Somehow, when I stopped hiding and being vague around money issues, I became clear about other areas of my life. Instead of acting out the ugly duckling I believed I was, I found that a beautiful swan had been there all along—strength, courage, and all.

If the saying "You have to lose a life to gain a life" is true, then I thank God for my new life.

Coming Out of Deprivation

This co-debtor came to D.A. because of "his problem"
and eventually came out of denial and deprivation.

I attended my first D.A. meeting because my husband had a debting problem. A couple of months before, he had confessed to having over $20,000 in credit-card debt, an amount, coming on top of huge student debts, that would be very difficult for him to pay off. He made that confession three days before our wedding, but I married him anyway. When I went to the D.A. meeting, I had run up a couple thousand dollars in debt on my own credit cards, supporting him. I wanted to learn from D.A. how to avoid being "codependent" with his debting.

I had been involved in other Twelve Step programs before. I did not think D.A. could be a program for me. I paid off my credit cards every month and had never in my life been extravagant with money. Quite the opposite, in fact.

I continued to attend D.A. searching for an answer to my co-debting, but I found myself strangely identifying with things said in the meetings. At one point a meeting needed a new literature person, and when no one else volunteered, I did. Two months later I returned to the meeting and I was asked for a literature report. I was stunned; I had forgotten about my service commitment! I offered to take on the position if they still wanted me. Thank goodness, they did. This service position kept me attending D.A. during a six-month-long period of denial during which I began to see my own debting disease with increasing discomfort. Every Wednesday before the morning meeting, I would say to myself, "I have no D.A.-related problem. I just go because of my service commitment. But it is another Twelve Step program, so it doesn't hurt me to go." And at every meeting after the standard readings, I would say to myself, "Oh yeah. I do belong here."

D.A. has been helping me heal from my own disease. Though I had never been extravagant in spending money, I had become ill in another, opposite way. For me it was as the "anorexic" is to the "overeater." I hoarded my money—every paycheck went straight into my savings account, with tiny amounts parceled out only as needed. I was very strict with myself. During a lean time some years ago, I managed to spend less than $5,000 in over six months. Since then, I've held that up as an ideal to which I fall short. I came to D.A. with a wardrobe utterly deficient in everything but business suits, because I found my job (i.e., the source of money) the only justification for spending on clothing. Soon after joining D.A., though I had paid off the credit cards and saved up substantial sums in the bank, my wardrobe remained unchanged. My underwear was in shameful condition; I had so few panties and bras that I had to wash them by hand every few nights. I owned only one pair of jeans, no dresses other than one that didn't fit and another that cost $3.00 at a garage sale. I had numerous shoes too ill-fitting or bizarre to wear because I had bought them thoughtlessly. They had been on sale, hard to resist with prices "slashed" by 70%. My remaining shoes were worn out. I used a watch-face which I kept in my pocket ever since the band broke. You get the idea.

The word for this is "deprivation." I lived in deprivation, deeply convinced of not "needing" anything more. Acknowledging any kind of "need" was unbearable for me. I didn't believe I deserved anything at all. That belief—that others deserve nice things but I do not—helps explain my otherwise uncharacteristic generosity to others with my money. Even most beggars I passed got money from me. A few years ago I spent nearly a month's salary on Christmas presents. When I first totaled up my spending records, I discovered that in one month I had spent $97.00 on beggars and charity, and $1.00 on entertainment for half the cost of a video rental. Then I realized I had to change.

I had other symptoms too. I so hated to part with my hoarded money that I paid all my bills late. I tended to "misplace" them, often receiving disconnection notices. I have always been vague about how much money I had in my stash, either dramatically overestimating or underestimating it, often by over half! In graduate school I once had to ask the university if I had paid that semester's $8,000 bill yet. I had a bank balance of $10,000 and didn't even know if I had $10,000 or $2,000 left for the rest of the year. That sort of thing happened frequently, because I was compulsively inattentive to my finances.

Time has been another big issue for me. I am a chronic "time debtor," creating chaos in my life by being vague about time. I underestimate how long it takes to get somewhere: I "forget" to go to bed early enough to get a good night's rest, wake up late, and suffer the "domino effect" all day. I am chronically late to appointments and Twelve Step meetings.

About eight months ago and after six months of faithful D.A. attendance, I broke through my thick denial, and a renaissance began for me. Today my old behaviors are far less frequent, and I feel less shame. I may occasionally forget how much money I have, but I have accurate records close at hand if I do. Miraculously, I even know how much money I spend per month and on what, so I know how much income I need. Right now I am looking for a new job, and I am demanding a much higher salary than I otherwise would, because I need it! And I even believe I deserve it. My list of belongings has expanded. I am approaching this Christmas with an awareness that I am "enough," and I do not need to buy love with generous gifts I cannot afford. Other kinds of new clarity are evident: I recently bought life insurance for myself and my husband. None of this has been easy; I nearly got sick to my stomach after I bought a nice watch for myself. Change never is easy, but, you know, it is worth it.

There's A Monster Living Inside Me

"When I lost my first tooth, the tooth fairy left an I.O.U. under my pillow."

There's a monster living inside me, and I call him "Not Enough." Every time I try to feed him he screams "I want more stuff!" A bike, nice clothes, new furniture, some pretty jewelry, vacations all around the world, all sorts of niceties. These things and more I've used to quench his beastly appetite. I finally shrug and tell myself I've tried with all my might. Then I plan to ignore him when he starts his usual stuff, but he screams more loudly "Hey! It's *you* who's 'Not Enough.'" My only ammunition in dealing with this jerk is what I call my Higher Power, and boy, does it work!! I say, "H.P., I need your help. Please shut up this big ape." H.P. sits me on his lap and asks, "Child, when will you see that the only way to quiet this goon is to fill him full of me!"

I now suspect the true monster was driving the first ten years of my life, which I remember as being very deprived. My father was in pharmacy school, while my mother worked as a secretary. We were on welfare, so poor that when I lost my first tooth, the tooth fairy had to leave an I.O.U. under my pillow. My parents had searched the house from top to bottom to find even a penny, and after a fruitless search between couch seats and car ashtrays, they had to leave an I.O.U. for me. My father borrowed a nickel from a classmate and placed it under my pillow the next night. Thus, my introduction to debting. Living under such deprived conditions, I was constantly aware of there not being enough.

Our basic living needs were barely met. This standard of living continued until my Dad graduated from college. We went from deprivation to abundance almost overnight. Suddenly there was money to spend frivolously. Throughout my adolescence I held various odd jobs, and just as soon as I got paid I spent my entire paycheck. When I'd ask my parents for more money, they would exclaim, "You just got paid; what happened to your paycheck?" I didn't have a clue where my money went. It just seemed to slip through my fingers. This vagueness was one of the main characteristics of my debting years. I never knew where my money went. I could withdraw $40 from the bank and the very next day be broke, wondering what had happened to it. And, I never learned the value of saving. It was as though there was a monster in me that needed immediate gratification. Tomorrow wouldn't do; the monster needed more and more, and it needed it *now*. I waited tables to put myself through college, all the while becoming more vague about my money.

I took out a student loan and was approved, but instead of using the money to cover living expenses, I squandered it on material things. Upon graduating from college, I was approved for two credit cards and thus began my descent into hell. I started charging things left and right, ignoring the bills as they came. Soon came the harassing phone calls from creditors. The phone became my enemy; I dreaded hearing it ring. I was so stressed out that I eventually wouldn't answer it, or I would answer and pretend to be somebody else. Now that's insanity...taking messages for myself to avoid dealing with reality!

Things went from horrible to excruciating until I finally decided to move across the country to "start new." In Twelve Step programs, this is known as a geographic cure. My parents, being enablers, refused to let me file bankruptcy though I was 27 at the time. They agreed to pay off my debt with the understanding that I would pay them back when I was able. I consented, but still moved from New Orleans to San Francisco to "start fresh." Although I was unable to accrue more debt from credit cards, I began to debt myself in other ways: underearning, underachieving, putting others' needs ahead of my own, while I neglected my own. I even "borrowed" from the treasury of the Twelve Step group I was doing service for. My "fresh start" soon became the same old, same old.

Finally I had had enough. I went to D.A. and sat quietly while others talked. I was amazed at how much I identified with those who shared. I began working my D.A. program. I felt like a newcomer, even though I had been clean and sober for over six years. I began writing down my daily expenses on the first of January, a few months after coming to D.A. I immediately noticed that the vagueness that had plagued me for years vanished. I began feeling hope.

I formed a Pressure Relief Group, and a most incredible miracle occurred: I quit worrying about money. Somehow I realized that I would be okay, one day at a time. My Higher Power is taking care of me, and as long as I continue to take action and do the footwork, I will make it through anything. Nine months after coming to D.A., I got a higher-paying job. I have been having regular

Pressure Relief Groups and have been participating in others since my third month in this program. I have approached my family to make amends for my debting. I've retired some debts. And I'm learning how to put my needs ahead of others, especially that "ogre that wants immediate gratification."

In a nutshell, I am learning how to be a responsible, productive adult human being for the first time in my life. D.A. is a program of action, and I have found that service work is a good way to keep me connected to the program; it keeps me active. This program has shown me that the universe is abundant and that I am worthy of my portion of that abundance: All I have to do is claim it! Lastly and most important, D.A. has reminded me of my visions and dreams for myself.

D.A. has given those back with the message that the only thing preventing me from realizing my dreams is me. The gratitude I have for Debtors Anonymous is enormous. Thank God for D.A.!

The Escape Artist

This debtor created only prisons until he learned to use the D.A. tools.

My problems with money literally began in my childhood, but I will fast forward to the summer after my thirty-third birthday. My girlfriend, whom I had become financially indebted to and dependent on, kicked me out. After the break-up of the relationship, a generous and compassionate friend took me into her one-room apartment. There I slept on the floor on a convertible mattress and tried to pull my life together during the day, while she was at work. I was a member of Al-Anon and A.A. and went to Twelve Step meetings day and night, just to keep from going out of my mind. You see, in addition to feeling devastated by the end of the relationship, I had no income except a modest unemployment check every two weeks. I had no money to move, to pay for rent, to pay for anything beyond groceries and transportation. I knew of D.A., but I was trying to hold on for dear life. Who had time for another Twelve Step program?

The only good news, or so I thought, was that I had moved, and none of my creditors knew where I was. You see, over the years I managed to accumulate more than 30 creditors to whom I owed more than $13,000. I was always temporarily relieved when I moved, which was frequently, and could escape the mail for a while. I got into debt by doing things like running up a long-distance phone bill for more than $1,000, not paying it, and then switching companies. I would also take out loans, embellishing the applications, to meet living expenses and spend the money rapidly without any means of paying them back. In addition, I hadn't paid taxes for five years, hadn't filed for an additional five years, and owed the government another $30,000 or so, and I got notices every month. I was definitely on the run. For the moment though, my friend's floor was the only place I had to go. The only solace I had was that very few people knew where I was. When they found me, I would ignore them.

It was hard to believe I was hiding again. I was used to it. My other Twelve Step experiences had yet to correct this character defect. Regarding money and responsibility, the mailbox had long been my enemy. Everyone wanted something I couldn't give. It got so I could not bear to go near the mailbox without intense fear. I actually accumulated over 175 pieces of unopened mail. I thought if I didn't open it, I was safe from problems I couldn't bear to face.

A week or two after moving in with my friend, I did begin, with great resistance, to look for work. I did so for more than two months, but the results were dismal and depressing. Maybe my attitude had something to do with it. My friend was clearly and understandably feeling the stress of having two persons in such a small space. I was in despair. I knew I could not stay with my friend indefinitely, but I couldn't afford to move. My job search was at a dead end. I needed money and time was ticking away. I have always been an escape artist, escaping every problem I've ever gotten into, but this one wasn't so easy.

Somehow I came up with the idea to make money for another getaway by holding a conference and charging people to attend. If successful, it would give me enough money to depart and find a little financial breathing space. Now in order to pull it off, I had to use my friend's phone constantly and turned her apartment into my office. In talking my friend into this arrangement, I was very convincing, like most escape artists. At this point, she grudgingly agreed, believing it would help me move out. Just about a week after I began working on this conference that would "save" me, the tension between us began to mount. I was doing my best to keep the activity in her apartment to a minimum, but the wheels were in motion for the conference. This continued for three months of constant phone calls, planning, papers everywhere. That I was overstaying my welcome is the understatement of the century. A combination of hard work and good luck made the conference a modest financial success. Looking back, I know my Higher Power was taking care of me.

As you might guess, the moment the conference was over, my friend, by now sitting on built-up frustration, asked when I was moving. In a sense, she became another creditor, wanting to know when was I going to take care of the problem. There was nowhere to run now; I was living with a "creditor." I felt a lot of pain and resentment toward her. I had not one second to enjoy my triumph, not one day to relax after the ordeal of the conference. My anger felt justified. My distorted thoughts told me that when I was down, people owed me a break, their understanding and compassion, though I gave little in return. How dare she take this attitude with me! In retrospect, I see how self-centered, arrogant and fearful I was. Now I had been asked by another woman to leave, just like my girlfriend before her.

This was a terrible reminder of how lost I was. Though I had a little money, I didn't know where I could go, because it wouldn't last. With no stable income and just a few strained friendships, it's no wonder why. I had no real prospects, my creditor and IRS problems were overwhelming, and I didn't know where to turn. The cumulative pain of all the years of running fell heavily upon me, and I could no longer escape. I felt tortured, and leaving this world crossed my mind.

Two days after my friend asked me to move, I somehow remembered D.A. A Twelve Step comrade had told me about D.A. many months earlier, and I had gone to one meeting then, but I thought "those people" were all nuts. Asking me to write down everything I spent! Sitting down with others and having them suggest how I should spend my money! Keeping records of whom I owe money to! I left that meeting saying that they were all "anal retentive." This time I went to meetings willing to listen. My intense pain had finally made me ready for something, anything. Desperation made me more reasonable. I now thank my Higher Power for this pain, because when I get crazy, and it still happens, pain makes me willing. Willingness has become the key to my recovery.

When I became willing to write down my numbers, translated to looking at the truth, I began to spend less. When I became willing to do spreadsheets, translated to identifying my true needs, I saw that I was not a compulsive spender. I discovered that I was not spending recklessly as I had believed, but had been underearning and couldn't meet my reasonable expenses. In fact, I was underspending in essential areas like the dentist, doctor, clothes, vacation, etc. Those things had been for others, not me. When I became willing to become solvent and stay that way no matter how scary, other options that I could have never dreamed of came to me. More than anything, when I became willing to go to meetings, make phone calls and listen to the suggestions from a Pressure Relief Group, my entire outlook changed.

Through the suggestions of a Pressure Relief Group, I began consulting with someone, charging them for my expertise. Though I had skills and talents to offer, I had been using them to scheme and get around life. Yet, this time I was using my assets with integrity. So I and my one client were going along fine, and I was doing office work and a few other things to make money. How convenient is my memory. I was also illegally on unemployment. I thought it was okay to collect unemployment and work "off the books" because I needed to survive. It kept me underearning and living on the edge, not helping my confidence one bit. But thankfully, I eventually got out of this trap. Here's how.

I was scrimping to get by, also working the program, but I wasn't willing to let go of my unemployment game. In a Pressure Relief Group I was asked if I was setting money aside for taxes from my consultant income. I was shocked. "I can't," I answered. I vaguely knew I should be setting aside a tax fund, but how could I when only making $50 some weeks? How could I take $15 of that and put it aside?

Under their gentle but persistent guidance, I agreed to take out 30% of every consulting check and set it aside for taxes, *no matter what*. I was afraid to do this with every bone in my body. I had hidden from the IRS for years, and there was no money to pay *Them*, the IRS, the bad guys. Now money I needed to live on was going to them. But as we discussed in the Pressure Relief Group, taking the money out was not only to stay out of tax debt, it was also to demonstrate my willingness for a Higher Power to replace it and somehow meet my needs. This was my first test of acting on faith, trusting the wisdom of others. After that, with each and every check, I kept 30% for taxes.

With this act of willingness, and others like it, my life changed drastically. I received more abundance than I believed possible. I am not even sure why. It's the demonstration of faith that made a difference. When I survived and more money began to come in through my actions, it seemed miraculous. Why, oh why, had I resisted for so long? Oh sure, I had fantasies of financial stability, but never really believed I could achieve financial comfort, pay off my debts, or stop living on the "edge." Maybe my Higher Power needed for me to learn something first and then by example, teach others. When I became willing to hold 30% and listen to the common wisdom of D.A., my life got better and better, and it still does.

Since coming into D.A., I have opened those stockpiled envelopes. Now I open my mail every day. I no longer fear, but actually look forward to my mail. By the way, inside two unopened envelopes were checks made out to me. Now I have filed all back taxes, and I am making an offer to the IRS to eradicate my debt. I pay quarterly taxes. I have paid ten creditors and make payments to others regularly. I know they will all eventually be paid. I have increased my income more than 75% over the last two years, and I save money every week. When I visited my family in the Midwest, I paid for my plane ticket and had the money to stay at a hotel, rent a car and even to treat my nieces and nephew.

Writing this brings tears to my eyes; because every year on every visit, I stayed at my parents' home, borrowed their cars and was ashamed about how little I had to spend. Now I could go home as an adult. My mother said to me, "How much is the plane ticket?" and I said, "Don't worry. I'm paying for it." She said, "Well, you know I can't come to see you in New York, so that's why your Dad and I send you money." "I know," I said, "but I'll take care of it. I'm fine. You spend it on yourself." She started to cry. Finally, money was not an obstacle between us. There was room now for feelings and growth. I can't overstate the power of this moment in my life.

My parents had come from Depression-era households. They never gave themselves much of anything and long suffered from financial and emotional deprivation. When, as a boy, I asked for 25 cents a week allowance, they said they couldn't afford it. Even then, I knew they could, but they were telling me there wasn't enough. My insanity with money and debt is evident in my belief that there isn't, and never will be, enough. My parents never felt they had enough. They couldn't give me what they couldn't give themselves—even 25 cents given with love and abundance was threatening. Willingness to come to D.A. and show up has released me from the corrosive and despairing attitudes my family and countless other families experienced.

From a poor, struggling household, from the floor of a one-room apartment, I have gone on to a great place to live, stable income, a thriving new business, and I move toward my vision proactively. I no longer wait for my money to run out before I take action. I have overcome, one day at a time, my almost terminal procrastination. My actions and money flow more freely. My creditors and Uncle Sam know where I live. I have six separate savings funds set aside for vacations, luxuries, investments, taxes, professional expenses, and a personal prudent reserve. I show up despite the fears that occasionally still run through me when I think it may all come to an end. The difference is that before D.A., things did run out: money, opportunity, friends, and love. Since D.A., abundance never runs out. In short, I have learned to begin taking care of myself. My other Twelve Step experiences are more rich when I keep the focus on myself. As I take care of what I can and leave the rest to my Higher Power, I have everything I need, and more. For the first time in my life, with D.A.'s help, today is much brighter and freer, and I look ahead to a promising future.

Even though I have been in other programs, I have never *felt* the existence of a loving Higher Power before. Now I do. Even when I struggle, I know I am being looked after. I know when I am willing, God makes all things possible. I still get angry, play out old habits, and I still have character defects, like intolerance, blaming, controlling or acting out of fear. Very recently I have taken time to pray for the people I resent or to affirm what I am grateful for so I don't hang on to the feeling. It's human to get angry, scared, judgmental, but I don't live in it. I learned much of this from reading the A.A. Big Book, something else I became willing to do.

I am truly grateful for what I have received since coming to D.A. I still have bouts with distressing feelings and self-centered fear, but I have others to help me get out of myself and into life. I have abundance, friends, greater feelings of self-worth and self-love—greater sense of purpose. I have more than enough money for today, and I have myself. Without D.A. I do not know where I would be, but now I know where I can go. Believe me, I was and still am afraid to try things that have been suggested. It's tough to leave all the familiar deprivation behind. With D.A., that is healing. Now I know that if I demonstrate my willingness, even the smallest amount, my Higher Power will lead me to abundance and grace. Whatever God is, God speaks through D.A. I am grateful I became willing to listen.

Busting Out of Debtor's Prison

*Expected crises were replaced with unexpected boons
as this member developed faith.*

I had bounced a rent check for the third time that year. The first two times, I had run to my parents with my tail between my legs to ask for help. As new grandparents of my infant son, they felt obligated to keep my head above financial disorder, though it was clear they were deeply concerned about why their thirty-eight-year-old son, a full-time assistant director of a college program, could not pay his own rent. Asking for money from them brought up tremendous shame for me, and I couldn't go back once again. I couldn't find a way to cover the two bounced checks. We had already borrowed from my wife's mother, and other family members and friends had their own financial troubles. I had reached the limits on my credit cards and could no longer turn to plastic as a way to come up with cash. My salary just didn't seem to keep up with my expenses.

As new bills came in from my therapist, the electric company, the gas company, the telephone company, two credit cards, department store charge cards. gas card, my student loan, my wife's student loan, and so on, I played a financial Russian roulette with my checking account, where I wrote checks based on money from checks that hadn't been cashed yet. I carefully calculated mail delivery and past cashing habits of the individuals involved. For example, my landlord rarely cashed a rent check before the last week of the month. When finally he did, it all crashed down on me, checks bouncing left and right, with no way to cover them and have food on the table. The angry phone calls increased. The bank fees I racked up on bounced checks alone were astounding and could have covered several of those bills.

I found myself scouring bookstores for self-help books on dealing with debts, and I found one that had only one suggestion for someone in my situation—Debtors Anonymous. After procrastinating for months and living in fear of answering my own telephone, I finally went to my first meeting on July 14,

1990—Bastille Day. I will always remember that date because it celebrates the destruction of a debtor's prison. And it was so clear to me too, when I heard what people in that room shared, that I belonged there. It was the first day I took a sledgehammer to break out of my own debtor's prison.

After going to six meetings, as suggested, I found a man and woman willing to do a Pressure Relief Meeting for me. In two Pressure Relief Meetings, they helped me look at my expenses and made it clear that I needed to increase my income to meet them. That made me angry, but I took their suggestions on faith and began to develop a willingness to look for ways to earn more income. Over the next two years, I took on various extra jobs doing classroom teaching, private tutoring, teacher training, and textbook reviewing. I also kept up with writing a textbook that I had already signed a contract to complete. After two and a half years, with the support of my program, my textbook review work led to a new job with a publishing company that paid more than I made in all other jobs combined, increasing my income from $29,000 when I began the program to $50,000 a year. This was someone who saw himself as never making more than about $35,000 a year!

Despite my salary increase, however, I tend to live on the edge. There never feels like enough. It feels that way because my disease puts me there. It is very difficult for me to put money in savings first—in other words, to take care of myself first. I spend what I have until the next paycheck comes, but with the support of the program, I am learning. Now I am taking baby steps to create a prudent reserve by setting aside a dollar a week in my wallet and five dollars a week in a savings account. In this program I have always found that baby steps are enough. When I remember to look back, I can see that they were not baby steps at all, but huge leaps.

I now know that I spent my first year in D.A. getting a handle on the tools of the program and my income and expenses. I did not pay anything to my creditors during that time, though I wrung my hands about it every day. It is clear to me now that I needed that time to get a sense of reality about what I need financially and what I could do to increase my income. A little over a year ago, I began paying my creditors small amounts, and since then I have never stopped.

I have been through the court process with three creditors and retired each of those debts, always taking care of myself first. With the help of my sponsor and pressure people, I learned to negotiate my way through garnishment of my wages, a freeze on my bank account, and court arbitration. I'll never forget arriving in an empty courtroom first thing in the morning and seeing the only words on the wall—In God We Trust. As a lifelong atheist, I had always felt threatened by that phrase. Now, thanks to the spiritual growth I have experienced in this program, it gives me great comfort

My creditors rarely call me, but when they do, I instinctively know what to say and do. I make no promises I can't keep, and I never make decisions I am not ready for without speaking to my sponsor or pressure people first. I pay what I can afford each month, and every month some write me to say the amount isn't acceptable. I know I cannot control their actions—that they have a procedure to follow—and now so do I.

It wasn't until my relations with my creditors became more manageable that I really began to discover the Steps of the program—the spirituality of the program—in a more conscious way. While I heard it countless of times in the rooms, "It isn't about the money," I never really understood until I got my financial feet on the ground. Now I wrestle with resentments, relationships, and other compulsions. Occasionally, money issues come back to haunt me. At one point I lost clarity about my checking account and came close to losing my solvency again. But I have found that the answer for me is always in the tools of the program. I look to see which tool I am neglecting. More often than not, it is my reading D.A. and A.A. literature or going to meetings. Meanwhile, this professed atheist prays every day for knowledge of God's will and the power to carry it out.

One of the first things I did when I began going to D.A. meetings was take full responsibility for myself as a compulsive debtor. I so wanted to include my wife in the equation. Hey, if you think I have a problem, what about her? But I had to let go. I remember coming home one day from a meeting and telling my wife that I was a compulsive debtor, the same way I would have told a close friend. From that day, I have chosen recovery, and my recovery comes first. I am fortunate my wife cooperated with me totally, even though she sometimes resents her loss of control over our finances.

One of my fantasies has long been that my wife would succeed in her chosen field, and there would be no pressure on me to do well in my career. As it turns out, my wife stopped earning money altogether, and I had to be the breadwinner—a role I resented. D.A. helped me take care of myself. Up to now that has included taking the steps I need to meet expenses and support a family. Only recently have I begun to look at my resentments at my wife for leaving me with total responsibility. Yet, I have learned the only answer is not living in the resentment, but cleaning up my side of the fence.

Until the time I came to D.A., my wife had handled most financial matters, particularly balancing our checkbook. She was good at math, and I believed I wasn't. I explained to her that for my recovery, it was important for me to get clarity and do all of these things for myself. Our checkbook, combined bills, and previously incurred debts have remained my responsibility since that time. I pay my wife an income every week for her services as homemaker. How she handles that money is her business, not mine. It was very difficult for me to let that control go. I feared that she would debt and drag me down with her, that she wouldn't buy enough groceries and I'd go hungry, that somehow she would do something that would interfere with my recovery. Since that time, she has incurred occasional small debts, but she has taken complete responsibility for paying them off. I have to admit that we have plenty to eat, though sometimes I feel deprived. She has not interfered with my recovery in any way, though my resentments often have. Acceptance has been very important to me in my marriage. I know that if I can't accept my wife as she is, I lose my serenity. That does not mean allowing her to interfere with my recovery, but it does mean stepping back and detaching with compassion when she is in the throes of her own stuff.

I wanted so much to believe that my crisis before July 14, 1990 was an aberration, just a "crisis." But looking back, I can see I have always had a problem with dependency on others, which manifested with money. I cringe at check-paying time in a restaurant, when there are others with me. One part of me wants to be an adult and pay my share; the other desperately wants someone else to treat, to take care of me, to give me a freebie.

I used to have a pattern of incurring debts to crisis proportions, then paying them off. Each crisis amounted to previously unthinkable amounts. One day it finally caught up with me. Right after starting my new job, something very interesting happened. One night, I went to a visions meeting because it was convenient to my train schedule. When I got there, there was no one to speak, so I volunteered. I had always hated visions meetings, because people always talk about how they are actors, singers or writers, but I had no idea if I even had a vision for my life. As I racked my brain thinking of what to share, I suddenly remembered a card where I had written some goals for myself. I had carried it around in my pocket for years. At that moment I realized that my written goals almost fit my new job to a tee. Though I hadn't had a vision with a title, I certainly had a vision of what I wanted to do. That experience tells me that it doesn't matter if recovery in D.A. feels like it is going right, or that I know I am doing enough, or that anything should be as I think it should be. Just by committing to working this program, using the tools to the best of my ability, recovery and the will of my Higher Power just unfold.

D.A. Recovery: Take Two

A debtor drives to the edge before turning back to D.A.

I came to Debtors Anonymous for the first time when I had six years of recovery in Alcoholics Anonymous, A.C.A., and Al-Anon. I was a divorced single mom of a seven-year-old boy and a full-time student at the local university. We were living on student loans, welfare and my part-time income. It was late summer, and we had just moved into a beautiful, roomy apartment, with a good friend as a roommate. Soon after that, I clearly heard little voices telling me it was all very nice, and we could lose it by Christmas. I talked about my fears of self-sabotage in A.A. meetings, and several people who were also in Debtors Anonymous started talking to me about D.A.

I began to attend meetings and knew this was the place for me, but I hated it. My experience with A.A. had been just the opposite. I had felt I was coming home and had found the first safe place in the world, maintaining sobriety from the first day I attended.

I began working with a Pressure Relief Group. Both people had over three years in D.A., old-timers in our area. I tried to do everything they suggested. My A.A. sponsor never had trouble with money, so I decided it would be all right to work my Steps around money issues with her. After all, she obviously had it together. She didn't disagree! I avoided the people I knew from my other program in D.A. meetings because I was "too embarrassed" to talk to them.

With the help of my Pressure Relief Group, I learned to keep records. I closed my checking account and used only cash because writing checks had no sense of reality for me. One day at a time I didn't incur new debt. I opened months of bills and notices from creditors. I organized everything in a notebook. My phone was cut off, and I borrowed from my boyfriend to have it turned back on. I hadn't ever told him how bad things were financially. He just knew things were tight because I was a student and a mom. I had never borrowed money from him in the three years we had dated, and I was ashamed to take money from him. I blamed my phone being cut off on my Pressure Relief Group.

Christmas came, and I had the most amazing holiday. I had virtually no money, and my Pressure Relief Group had me meditate each day on what my Higher Power would have me write down as gifts for people on my list. My son ended up receiving everything on the list from other people, and I wasn't able to buy him one of those things. It was a humbling lesson for me about not being the Source.

Another surprise was a marriage proposal from my boyfriend. I was very happy when I came to my next Pressure Relief Group with the news. They were supportive and helped me prepare to tell him about my financial history. I wanted him to see it all before we got married. We started to work on my spending plan. They also suggested my fiance come to a Pressure Relief Group, so we could plan our non-debting wedding together. That was my last meeting with them.

Two and a half years later, I was sitting on a curb outside an A.A. meeting sobbing about how suicidal I was feeling. The friend I was talking to patted me on the back and said, "I think you need to go back to D.A. I think you missed something important the first time."

I came back to D.A. convinced I was going to die. During my two-year debting spree, I had been employed in the profession I had studied for and made good money. But we were thousands of dollars deeper in debt than when we had married. We had credit cards. We lived from cut-off notice to cut-off notice. We were behind in our rent. And then, I lost my job. The balls we were frantically juggling all dropped and went careening wildly in all directions. I couldn't breathe. I couldn't eat. I couldn't find a job. I was immobilized most of the time.

I approached D.A. differently this time around. I immediately made a service commitment. I found a D.A. sponsor and began working the Steps. I went to every meeting I could. I called people. My daily terror increased dramatically as I made the commitment not to debt, one day at a time. The first woman I asked to sit on my Pressure Relief Group said she would, but she needed me to know she had filed bankruptcy in D.A.; it had been the correct thing for her. I couldn't have cared less about why she thought it was important for me to know that. I just needed to do everything suggested so I wouldn't die!

Powerlessness and unmanageability were not difficult to admit. I felt completely abandoned by my Higher Power, so walking through Steps Two and Three was arduous. The morning I was finally able to make the decision to turn my will and my life over, I prayed in front of the little altar in our bedroom.

I acknowledged the desire to know my Higher Power and committed to working the rest of the Steps to complete my spiritual awakening. I humbly prayed, "I know you are the Source. Please, show me how to accept what you have to give. Show me how I can best be of service to my world. I know I am a channel, not the Source." There was a lightening of my entire being. A couple of minutes later I was headed downstairs when my husband walked in the front door with the news, "Honey, I quit my job." My first reaction was, "He isn't the Source either." I had a day of complete peace. My terror returned the next day, but I had done my Third Step and nothing could remove the impact of that decision.

By the time I had completed my inventory and was trying to share it with my sponsor, it was clear I could no longer work with her. I was grateful for the time we had spent. She had clarified so much about what brought me to D.A. I wasn't finding anyone else I wanted to work with, and sitting on my completed Fourth Step was making me nuttier than I already was. There wasn't much room for decline! After having her name come to me several times while praying for help, I did my Fifth Step with a program friend who is a therapist. She is well-acquainted with D.A. and incest recovery. She also helped me with my list of outdated survival skills that were surfacing at the beginning of my Step Six.

A week or so later, I was in the town eight miles north of where I lived. I knew I would drive off the freeway and kill myself if I tried to go home. I was able to get to the local mental institution. They invited me to stay, but I refused. They treated me for anxiety and depression, and I went home. I began to work with a therapist on my chronic depression and anxiety. I had lived with them all my life and didn't know. I took medication for eight months to help relieve the symptoms. It enabled me to finally dive into the deepest core of my experience, feelings I had not been able to touch in my nine years of Step work and therapy.

About a month after my close call with suicide, I had the opportunity to attend the D.A. World Conference. My husband went with me, hoping to hear something that would help him, but he didn't think he had anything in common with anyone there. I absorbed the entire day. My soul stirred when I heard one woman speak on the Visions panel. Next week I tracked her down and asked her to be my sponsor. She lived 40 miles away, but I was willing to go anywhere to work with her. She asked for time to pray about it and called a few days later, agreeing to sponsor me. Then we met for the first time. Our long-distance relationship has worked well, and we have continued even though she now lives in another state.

I spent my first two years in almost daily terror. Things looked worse financially. We went deeper into debt. Work was sporadic and unpredictable for both of us. My compulsions got much worse, and I injured myself at work. Our home was not a pleasant place most of the time.

By continuing to work the Steps, work with my sponsor and my Pressure Relief Group, go to meetings, talk to people, and make friends in D.A., I have learned to see how my basic needs are being met each day. When I project ahead one bit, I fret and worry, and sometimes quickly, sometimes slowly, end up in terror again. I know I don't need to act on anything when I am feeling urgency.

I have had a very difficult time with my faith. It finally occurred to me a few months ago that I didn't see or feel the same about anything anymore, but I was waiting to have the same comfortable feelings about my Higher Power that I had in my first years of recovery. Since that day, I have just prayed to please be shown what I need to see and to feel what I need to feel. I didn't know how it should be. The wonderful woman who sat on my Pressure Relief Group for over two years constantly urged me to go inside to learn what was correct for me. My sponsor told me it is my responsibility to check within before making decisions. Now I have learned how to identify some of my needs, accept them, and act on getting them met.

Both people who now sit on my Pressure Relief Group are able to accept abundance in most areas of their lives. I want to believe I deserve abundance too. My husband started attending D.A. nine months ago, and we have been current on all bills for five months. We have a goal to begin debt repayment this year. Our home is loving and supportive, and our family flourishes. We started a D.A. Couples Meeting in our home. I am still disabled from my work injury, but my sponsor keeps reminding me this is a gift of time. I recognize that at times, and I am grateful. I am taking art classes for the first time in my life and exploring new career opportunities.

Maybe it is because I am a recovering alcoholic/addict, but I was not able to fully commit to D.A. recovery until my behavior became life-threatening. On the days I don't want to keep going, I have the day I couldn't get on the freeway to look back on. I know I can only go forward or I will die, so I keep taking each small step. I am learning I don't have to do things alone. D.A. is teaching me to find and accept all kinds of support. I try to treat myself in a loving way each minute of every day. And I try to treat all others the same way. I am so thankful for the Steps, tools and people of D.A. They have saved me and given me a rich life.

I Can Relate

*He was an auto mechanic with a two-digit bank balance
before he found hope in D.A.*

I had a job that paid well for a blue collar mechanic, and all I knew was a few days after I received my direct deposit stub, the numbers in my checkbook would be down to three digits, usually two. Unexpected or ignored expenses like property tax, dental, medical, or repair work would usually end up on plastic or not done at all.

I had sold a rental and refinanced and consolidated loans, swearing never again. I hated numbers, money, my job, my life, my wife, and anything that made me write a check.

I picked up the seldom-read local paper, not looking for anything in particular, when the three-line ad jumped out at me

Debtors Anonymous.
There is hope.
Call _____.

From previous experience, I knew what "anonymous" meant, and I knew the power of Twelve Step groups. I trembled as I dialed the number and got a message giving meeting times and places.

Sneaking out of work a little early, I found the meeting place, sat down, and waited and waited. Nobody showed up. It must have been the night to stay home and pay bills I thought, as I walked into another ongoing Twelve Step meeting down the hall. I sat there quietly, feeling really betrayed and alone. Many people there mentioned money, but had no solutions.

The next D.A. meeting was five long days away, giving me time to work through most of my initial animosity and show up with a fairly open mind. At first I was too numb and apprehensive to get much out of the sharing, but I heard hope, honesty, a lot of my own story, and people being applauded for buying new underwear. I heard strange words like pauperism, Pressure Relief Groups, and spending plans. To some of the people, I couldn't relate. Many were new, unemployed, or grossly underemployed, divorced, bankrupted at least once and driving around in nine-year-old vehicles looking for work. Those that were prosperous praised the D.A. program like TV evangelists, sharing almost unbelievable tales of recovery using the tools of D.A. and the Twelve Steps.

So I went to meetings, kept track of my spending, and found about 25% to 30% of my take-home was vanishing every month. I thought I had a good handle on those things called codependency and denial, but numbers don't lie.

My wife and I agreed to separate both the bills and our incomes, paying equal shares according to our income, leaving both of us with money for what we both wanted. I trusted as always that all bills were being paid, and no new debt was being incurred.

Within a year I was able to go on vacation paying for everything with cash. It was great. After vacation I had enough in my tool and equipment fund to pay cash for a nice-sized new metal lathe and accessories, something I had only dreamed of for years. Had I arrived?

A couple of months later, all hell broke loose. Disconnect notices, telephone calls from creditors I'd never heard of wanting immediate payment, irritating phone calls from a gravelly voiced Mr. _____, informing me I was twenty days late on my payment again. I was about to experience the effects of credit codependency in a community property state.

Trying to salvage what was left of our credit, I kept in contact with all the creditors, relying on our joint income. But the other part of the "joint" wasn't there, and communications soon got nasty with threats of liens, garnishment of wages, and a lawsuit in progress.

The first Monday in October, 1991 I was asked to pick up one of my employer's mid-management people at the airport. He looked a bit sad and very serious. As I turned onto the freeway, he said to me, "Bad news, D_____, the company is having a mass layoff. This envelope contains a letter of explanation and a severance check. I'll need to have you turn in all company books, property, credit cards, and company truck. I'm sorry. This was a shock to me too."

I was a bit irritated. Six more months, and I would have been fully vested in the profit sharing. After the initial sinking feeling, a D.A. calm came over me. I felt okay. There was enough time and money. I didn't need to get hasty. In the back of my mind I was ready. After being employed by this big sick company for six and a half years, I was ready for anything. After my special company tools, books and credit cards were turned in, I made an offer on the company truck and drove it home.

The next night as I walked into a D.A. meeting not really knowing my next move, one of those little voices in the back of my head said, "You're going to be an independent repair mechanic," and I knew then this was what I had been preparing to do for years.

Within 15 days I was licensed, insured, and in direct competition with my old employer. Before the end of the month, my business cards were ready, and customers were calling. People were paying me a buck a minute to do just what I wanted to do most: repair machines.

My first year self-employed as a corporation was not all roses. The recession hit hard. Personal bankruptcy and divorce sidetracked me for a while. Numerous Fourth and Fifth Steps on fears, resentments, and social behavior, and cleaning up as much wreckage of the past as I could, as quickly as I could, saved my butt.

As this year draws to an end, my new marketing plan is slowly taking shape for the coming year and beyond. If all goes well, and I know it will, I'll be forming a second corporation with a very talented soul within the next six months.

Ask me if I can relate, as I drive around in my eight-year-old pickup looking for work and talking to a customer on my cellular phone. You bet I can. Thanks, D.A.

A Storybook Credit Card Debtor

His mother gave him his first credit card and his first D.A. meeting.
He did the rest.

I've often thought that the events that brought me to D.A. were not gory enough. After I got to the program, I heard people talk about being arrested, garnishment, repossessions, and judgments from credit card companies. My circumstances seemed to pale in comparison to those stories. Somehow I'm sure now that the degree of gore is irrelevant. What is relevant is whatever got you to D.A. and keeps you coming back.

I was a storybook credit card debtor. My mother gave me my first credit card shortly before I went off to college. Even though the card was on her account, I started charging recklessly. I loathed paying her for things I charged. After college, I began accumulating department store credit cards and major credit cards of my own. I got a great job, a nice apartment, new friends, and yet, I was miserable. Earlier that year, I had revealed my sexual orientation to my mother. We went through a very difficult time exchanging hateful comments and accusations. By the time graduation rolled around, I had put my sexuality on the back burner, but the pot was slowly coming to a boil.

That summer the pot boiled over. My father died suddenly, which sent me into a near-catatonic state. A few days after the funeral, my mother, frustrated by the silence, told me she was glad my father never knew of my homosexuality. She said that he never would have been able to deal with it, and if he had not died of a heart attack, my being gay would have killed him for sure. The saddest thing of all is that I believed her.

Strangely enough, although looking back maybe it wasn't so strange that month was the first time I received a credit card bill of my own. After all those years of never seeing the actual bill from my mother's account, I discovered that credit card companies did not, in fact, require you to pay in full, as my mother had. The words "minimum payment" became music to my ears and a new way of life.

Four years later, when I realized I could no longer meet even minimum payments on my credit cards, I panicked. It took effort to make sure my mother never knew of my difficulties. I got a second job to help catch up on my bills. I stopped going out completely. I figured I was safe if I stayed home locked in my apartment, far from the lure of using my credit cards for clothes that didn't fit, gifts for people, or things I didn't need. I figured it was a kind of punishment for all the debting I had done. I sidestepped all conversations about money, and I didn't answer the phone before 9 p.m. I threw all my unopened bills into a shopping bag. I was sure I could clean up my mess, or better yet, I would wake up one day and the mess would be gone.

Months later I was awakened by my mother calling to tell me that one of my creditors had called her to collect money, because I had not responded to their calls or correspondence. I was devastated. I felt ashamed. Now I had my mother on my back, which scared me more than any creditor could. More humiliation followed when, at my mother's insistence, I flew home, carrying my shopping bag full of unopened bills, to go to our local town bank so she could co-sign a loan to pay off my debts. I was mortified when my mother said to the bank office, "If he's even one day late on the payment, call me. Don't even bother calling him."

I handed over eighteen credit cards to my mother and kept one for emergencies (Ha!). I told my mother it was in her best interest to let me keep one major credit card to charge airline flights. In the event of my death, she would be the beneficiary of $300,000 from a life insurance policy I got when I charged flights. With the money from the loan my mother co-signed, all my creditors were paid off. Now I had only one payment to make to the bank. I felt naked. Within a month, I had called six of my old creditors to get new cards. For the next year and a half, I rode the debting roller coaster. All I had to do was make sure I paid the bank on time. My other six creditors didn't have my mother's address or phone number, so I was safe. Soon enough, I was clothed with guilt again. Creditors were calling me at work. I was placed in collections and written off by a few. All my credit cards were at or near their maximum. I used to sit up at night at my kitchen table smoking cigarettes and fantasizing about winning the lottery. I used to try to figure out who I would pay off first.

When the phone company shut me off for non-payment, I had to go to the business office to pay the bill. I stood in line in my suit, crisply starched shirt, and my perfectly scrubbed exterior and listened to other unfortunate people explain why they could not pay their bills. I couldn't believe they could make up such lies. When the service representative told me they would turn my service back on without a security deposit because I had been such a good customer I was thrilled. I smugly replied that I was glad she noticed. I added, "Why, I could have put a child through college on what I've paid the phone company. At least I feel better that I didn't make up a story why I couldn't pay like the other people here today." I was so proud of myself, I went to the nearest department store and charged something.

A few months later, I was finally cut off from writing checks at the grocery store. That had been my last salvation. The next day my mother called. The bank had finally called her, because I had been late on the loan payment for nine months in a row. Oddly enough, my mother didn't yell or scream or say anything nasty. She did tell me she wouldn't help me out this time. She asked me if I knew about Debtors Anonymous. I had seen a meeting notice in a community calendar for a D.A. meeting on Fridays for the past two years. Then she asked if I wanted to go to a meeting now, and I said yes. She said, "If you go to D.A., I'll leave you alone. I can't help you anymore, but I think D.A. can."

I wanted to hang up fast and race to that meeting, except it wasn't Friday! The magic words my mother said kept ringing in my ears, "If you go, I'll leave you alone." It was worth going just for that. For an instant, I was angry that she hadn't offered to pay off the loan, but from the very first minute I walked into D.A., I realized my mother had done me a favor by not bailing me out. In D.A. I heard the same stories with different sets of circumstances, some worse, some better, some about the same. I also heard people talking about their visions, and the steps they were taking to do things in abstinence. What I saw, however, was more important. I saw people at peace.

After a while, things began to get better. I heard fantastic slogans like, "I am not my debt," and "I owe my creditors money, not my self-respect." I had regular Pressure Relief Groups, and I gave Pressure Relief Groups. I did the actions on my action plan. I did service in meetings, and eventually I managed the D.A. phone in our city. I was always stunned when people approached me after meetings and said, "You were the voice on the phone. You listened to me and didn't tell me I was stupid or bad that I had gotten into debt. My life is so much better since I got to D.A." I always thanked them and added, "That was God's voice on the phone, not mine."

When I did my first Fourth Step, my mother's name came up all over the place. I kept going back to read my favorite story in the A.A. Big Book "Doctor, Alcoholic, Addict." I loved reading over and over, "If you had a wife like Max, you'd drink too." It was exactly how I felt about my mother. For years, I had told my friends, my family, and just about anyone who would listen how crazy my mother was. Who could blame me for being such a mess? When I was a teenager, my mother told me I'd probably grow up to be an alcoholic. I guess I showed her; I did everything else but drink!

What my first inventory revealed, and what nearly every inventory has revealed since then, is quite simple. The exact nature of my wrongs was not my mother, my dead father, my sister, my brother, my aunt, my uncle, my lovers, my friends, my bosses, my creditors, my sexuality or anything else that was put in my path. It was me, and how I reacted. It was my inability and unwillingness to live a spiritual life, spiritual laziness.

I felt, after a year or two, that the compulsion to debt using credit cards and other forms of unsecured debt had been lifted. Now when I am afraid to look at my checkbook, hesitate to spend money in one of my categories, or don't total my numbers for a few months, I go back to the basics and the spiritual principles of the program. Working D.A. when there are no crises to manage is hard only when I try to do it alone.

I have often thought that years ago I must have a dug a deep hole and buried all my visions in that hole. Every charge, every bad check I wrote, every resentment I had toward someone else, and every gossipy word out of my mouth was like throwing a shovel of dirt on top of those visions. Working the Steps and doing a Fourth Step is like digging out of the hole one shovelful at a time. Sometimes the dirt falls back into the hole, and I have to dig out again. Sometimes the visions are buried so deeply that I have to jump into the hole to carry them out gently with my hands. I think sharing this process with other people who are doing the same thing is what makes it work.

One of the visions that is materializing for me is figure skating. I started skating when I was eight. I was the only boy in our town who did figure skating, so I was harassed a lot. I skated in the local ice shows, and I eventually skated a solo and did some ice dancing. When I was seventeen, I stopped skating. To continue would have required money and time. For fifteen years I told people that I stopped because my mother wouldn't pay the money. I now know that was a lie. I stopped because I was scared. In fact, I never even asked my mother for the money. I just assumed her answer would be no.

Over the years I skated occasionally, but never attempted a jump, spin or dance pattern. Last year I tired of skating around the rink without doing anything. I realized with the help of my program that if I didn't do something, I would die spiritually. I started lessons again and bought a pair of expensive skates. I had skating as a category in my spending plan. I go to skating events and watch them on TV, all extremely painful for me before D.A. I'm learning dance patterns and have again started to jump and spin. Sometimes I am still afraid to fall or I feel intimidated by other skaters. I have a spiritual strength I didn't have when I was seventeen.

As my visions unfold, I have held onto one thought—that visions are not about my job, my apartment, my car, vacations, my new relationship with my mother, or even figure skating. Visions for me are about balance, balance with God and the world around me. In D.A., I've attained what I consider material prosperity as well as great spiritual and emotional prosperity. I used to say in D.A. meetings that my car made my heart sing or skating made my heart sing. Now I feel that being balanced is what really makes my heart sing.

Higher Power is Driving

She wanted somebody else to take care of her.
She knew she couldn't do it herself.

The story of my life in D.A. is one that is still unfolding. I have only begun to identify the ways I am changing now: the illumination, the burdens made lighter, paths made clearer. But I am a willing participant in this discovery process.

First and foremost, the tenth and eleventh *Signposts On the Road To Becoming a Compulsive Debtor* have been true for me since childhood: First, I believed that someone else would take care of me, so I wouldn't have to. I believed I was not capable of taking care of myself. Throughout my eight years of college, I never gave a thought to what my earning capability would be, nor did I ever speak to anyone about a career path. I was and am now an artist, and that is all I ever wanted to be. When a lucrative and viable career in commercial art came my way, I frustrated hopeful employers with my lack of ambition, squandering opportunities that others would have treasured. I was emboldened to leave the field altogether when I met the man who would become my husband. He struck me as a strong candidate for rescuer and caretaker of me and my stray life, despite the fact that he was broke and rootless himself, a stray seeking some sort of refuge.

Through the years we've been married, we have racked up around $25,000 of debts on eleven credit cards. We've lived penniless and homeless, bought and lost a home in foreclosure, bought another home, and gone through 26 automobiles, to name a few of our trials and inanities. I now see my use of credit cards was an act of aggression toward my husband, punishing him for not taking care of me. Never once in my debting days did I give a thought to paying the money back.

My husband's debting was motivated by his own issues, which I have learned are not for me to judge or analyze. I am responsible for my own lot in life, and the good and bad of it has come to me because of who I am. I would love to blame my husband for our debt problems, but fortunately now understand the relationship between taking responsibility and accepting my life so I can make the most of my gifts.

My first discovery in D.A. was my belief that if I ignored my problems they would cease to exist. I came into the program at a time when I had decided to take the family finances back into my own hands. In desperation my husband had been throwing the unopened bills into a cardboard box. The job of sorting and clarifying our debts was enormous. The job of contacting each creditor was even bigger, and it was extremely emotional and exhausting. But the payoff in D.A. was regaining my dignity as I faced reality, when the cloud of vagueness began to fade away.

I did my initial work with the help of program calls and a few meetings. Then, I thought I had everything under control and quit D.A. I thought my involvement in another Twelve Step program would address any issues that could come up. Six months later I found myself even more desperate and confused, and I was finally graced with the willingness to make D.A. a living part of my life.

Since that time, I have discovered a fellowship of loving, accepting support and help available in D.A. through meetings, personal contacts, sponsors, Pressure Relief Groups, and phone calls to members. I never cease to be amazed by the spirit of service that is alive in this program. It truly seems to be the case that members get as much out of helping others as they do out of being helped.

For me, the most important part of the program is learning to recognize my Higher Power's presence in my life, and coming to believe I am taken care of, with all my needs met; that I will not be abandoned; that I can dispense with the homelessness contingency fantasies. It is not my husband or my father who is my provider. All abundance, goodness, and wealth are from God.

Here is an example of God' s presence in my life today: My cars are falling apart, and we don't have the money to repair them, a familiar situation. I have prayed for a car and wondered how long I could go on like this. My mother offered to lend me her car while she is away, which is great. Today I got a call from a friend who shared the good news that she'd just taken a temporary job out of state, but she needs to do something with her car while she is gone. Not only can we help one another, but she just happens to leave on the day my mother returns!

Today I'm grateful to be alive. I accept my husband and myself as children of God. I am grateful for the trials I've had to face, for they have shaped and strengthened me. I am willing to do whatever my Higher Power places before me, whether that means speaking up honestly to my loved ones about difficult issues, getting a job, taking a rest, or reaching out for help. Today is a beautiful day, and I have everything I need.

The Adventure of the Divine Design

What she learned at home, church and school drove her crazy.
In D.A., she learned sanity.

Once upon a time I was a little Princess living happily ever after. I was surrounded with love, dancing and playing without a care. My wonderful family surrounded me, and I was as happy as a five-year-old heart could be.

Then my dear, loving grandfather died and left me. My father's alcoholism progressed, and he left me. My mother's suicidal depression and drug dependency swirled around me, and I was left vulnerable and unprotected to face repeated molestation and sexual abuse from both a neighbor and my Christian school bus driver. Being raised in the fundamentalist Brethren Church, I believed that Satan was in me, and that I must really be a bad person. My perpetrator told me I "owed" him. By the time I left third grade, I had learned the philosophy that would guide my life: I owed everyone and didn't deserve success at anything.

From third grade on, I remember there being a total lack of pleasure in my life. Everything was extremely serious, no humor. My mother was incapable of nurturing—no hugging, no kind voice, no hope through words. Nothing. My life was devoid of joy. The focus was on my alcoholic father, praying for his return.

Ours was the only divorced family in our church/Christian school, so we were ostracized in numerous subtle ways. I tried, but I could never measure up without a father in our home. I learned that without a man in your life, you were nothing. I learned that men couldn't be trusted, but then neither could women. I learned that if God was punishing us, we must have done something wrong. Life was full of tears, all black and white.

When I was fifteen, I fell in love. His family wasn't divorced, he seemed loyal, a good member of the church. I thought, "Here's a man that will never leave me." I was going to be smarter than my mother. I wasn't going to marry the type of man she did. I was wrong.

Things were unraveling by the time I graduated from high school. My brother was using drugs, shoplifting, and running an insurance scam. My sister was indulged and spoiled. I was teaching Bible lessons to five-year-olds in our Christian Sunday school. Our home was a constant battle.

Then I became pregnant. My mother, a registered nurse, didn't know about it, even though I was living with her up until I gave birth. Denial! To help cover up the pregnancy, I ate and ate, gaining 90 pounds. My boyfriend became more and more distant, and I slipped into loneliness and despair.

A week after my daughter was born, we married. We tried to live like Lucy and Ricky, but neither of us had parenting or communication skills. He worked all the time; I cried a lot, ate, and spent money. We just pretended our problems were behind us.

Within six months of our marriage, my husband went to Vietnam. He returned without a job and no self-esteem. He took a job below his skill level, because he had to support his family. His resentment put a barrier between us, so when I tried to reach him, he was emotionally abusive. He wanted to kill me, and I didn't know what to do. In response, I went on rampages of eating and spending, gaining huge amounts of weight and spreading hot checks all over town.

To earn his love, I would lose 100 pounds and try to be "perfect." Once I got my weight down, my check writing would take off. Then I'd get the money under control and binge on food. I kept repeating this cycle. I would chase the money, chase the marriage, and chase love, but I couldn't get them together at the same time.

By now I had two children, and we were getting involved again with our church, looking for the peace and happiness that we both desired. Since I was working, my husband decided to go into business for himself. His main account was my brother.

My brother was involved with a variety of underworld people, and so the money poured in. Greed was everywhere around us, but the money made it all right. When it began to fall apart, my husband became increasingly more abusive.

My brother got into a bit of trouble and torched his business to collect insurance money. Now he went underground to hide from the mob. In this, my husband saw a window of opportunity. He developed the contacts my brother had and became involved in a car theft ring and freight robbery. He began drinking heavily and seeing women on the side. My church told me I needed to be a supportive wife and that I was to offer this man a "refuge." We separated seven times in two years. I wanted to do what "God" wanted me to, but I could not stand the pain.

Finally my husband began to have trouble with the mob. Two thugs with guns came to the house looking for him one night, one at the front door and one at the back. My two children were asleep inside, and I panicked. I managed to get rid of the two men, because I didn't know where my husband was.

A few days later, I opened our garage to discover it full of hijacked dryers. My husband had hit the wrong truck, and the mob wasn't happy. No one in our family or our church would believe me when I told them, so no one would help. They told me one more time that my husband needed a "refuge," and a wife should provide that. I went into a rage, and that was the end of our marriage.

For the next week all I could do was lie on the floor beside the bed and cry. I decided that I was going to die. I told God I was coming to see Him and released my spirit. I remember my spirit, as it began rolling out of my body. Then I saw a large white being at my feet saying, "I'm sorry, but it's not time yet." I screamed "I want to die! I'm going to die!" But I didn't die; I've stayed here.

I found Adult Children of Alcoholics, Debtors Anonymous, Overeaters Anonymous, Alcoholics Anonymous, and eventually Co-Dependents Anonymous. My first year I couldn't do anything but go to meetings, therapy, and bed. My whole belief system had unraveled, and I was being put back together. I was being re-parented by the program.

My mother stopped talking to me because I left the church, and she considers Twelve Step programs to be cults. That has been really painful, but I'm here for myself. This is where my answers lie. If she chooses to not be in my life, I accept her decision.

For my first few years in recovery I remember the incredible pain of coming out of denial. I began participating in life, some good, some bad, but all of it was growth. I decided I really wanted a college education. I wanted to learn to connect my thinking and my feelings. I wanted to know if the things I had intuitively known in business were valid. Attending college was a financial struggle. I even lost my house in foreclosure, but I stayed focused on my dream and graduated. I eventually discovered there was a validity for the way I did business. I wasn't crazy; I was intuitive.

After I graduated, I began to repay my debts. It took me a year of hard work, but I paid off everything. I earned my freedom! What glorious freedom!

I had discovered a wonderful secret during one of my Pressure Relief Groups. I knew I didn't like "work," and that I didn't want a "job." Those words gave me such a negative image that I had resisted them even before I knew what "they" were. My Pressure Relief Group suggested that I needed a "money making play thing," or "MMPT" as I now call it. It was a wonderful idea. "Work" and "jobs" can become fun when they're money making play things. That I can do!

The biggest thing I learned through this whole recovery process was that I'm not crazy. It was the system I came from, not me!

Today I'm on to my next adventure. When you clear out the wreckage, you can enjoy the adventure of life. Different issues still come up, but there are no accidents. There is a divine design, and it's up to me to lean into it. Yes, the program has also given me a new Higher Power that I call Emmanuel. Today I have spirituality and joy in my life. Today I feel incredibly happy and rich, and I know that's the way it's supposed to be.

Going to Any Lengths for My Vision

*After workaholic debting and illness, D.A. helped her discover
that both her spirit and her health required balance.*

I was the kind of person who for many years said of Debtors Anonymous. "At least there's one Twelve Step program I don't need." I first came into recovery as a low-bottom alcoholic and drug addict. I knew I needed help, and A.A. was the answer, no question. Later I found relief with Cocaine Anonymous, discussing those parts of my life that I did not feel comfortable airing at A.A. meetings. Next, it became clear that I was using food in the same ways I had used drugs, so I trudged the happy road into Overeaters Anonymous. Over the years I added Co-Dependents Anonymous, Workaholics Anonymous, and Sex and Love Addicts Anonymous to my repertoire. In every case, there was no doubt in my mind that I had a problem ripe to be addressed by the anonymous program in question. I was served well by these programs and am grateful to them all. And yet, after eight years of glorious recovery, I found myself in the most enormous and seemingly intractable pain. How did I get here?

First let me tell you why I thought I didn't qualify for D.A.. Ever since I was as young as I can remember, I liked money. Liked to receive it, count it, save it, hide it, steal it, cheat my siblings out of it, keep track of it, and sometimes spend it. Not that I had a whole lot, but I sure knew what I did have. I had a savings account from the time I was in junior high school and thrilled to see how my balance increased without my doing a thing. I loved interest! In high school I began dealing drugs and kept scrupulous records of my investments and profits. At college I opened a checking account. From the beginning, I kept it balanced to the penny. It never occurred to me to do otherwise. It was inconceivable that I trust the bank to keep track of my money, or risk bouncing checks and pay service charges. In fact, for many years when there was a discrepancy between my records and the bank records, more often than not, the bank had erred. Oh, was I righteous! In college I also kept records of my expenses, both cash and checks.

I loved knowing where every dollar was spent. It gave me a feeling of being in control. I did not like being vague.

I resisted getting a credit card at first, because the idea of paying interest galled me. I was finally convinced by the conventional wisdom that said you need a credit history. "Okay." I thought. "If that's part of the program, I'll go along. But I'll do it my way." I got a bank credit card. Every time I used it, I sent a check to cover the amount of purchase immediately, long before the bill came. For years I never had to pay interest. I had beat them at their game. I had no problem with money.

I finished college and began a free-fall into full-time drug dealing and using. Within a year I had stopped eating well, sleeping enough, and swimming. When I ran out of money, I bounced checks, living off my credit cards until they were taken away. My accounts were turned over to collection agencies. When I surfaced in brief periods of lucidity, I'd set up payment schedules with agencies and even stick to them. It was not even arduous for me.

When I came into A.A. recovery, I got back on a meticulous record-keeping track and paid back my outstanding institutional debts, though I did not touch the $10,000 I owed to various drug dealers. You see, my problem wasn't money. I was an out-of-control drug addict. I didn't need D.A.

I had a job that paid me well and provided juicy benefits. Among them was health insurance, which I used to clean up the physical wreckage of my past. I hated the job. I worked my way from receptionist to account executive of a graphic design subsidiary of the largest advertising firm in the world. Trying to convince prospective clients to use my company to design their mayonnaise label was worse than useless. It was repugnant to me, for I had strong moral and political beliefs against commercial advertising. Working for the industry meant I was supporting it and was helping engender the problems it creates. What kept me there were money, benefits, and my belief that you can't get paid well doing "Good Works." By that I meant working for social justice, peace, political change, or non-profit causes.

I am an infinitely creative being with lots of support, and I need not be bound by convention or habit or mass mind or social pressures. Further, I recognize that what I assume will happen or expect is more likely to happen than what I do not assume or expect. My mental energy contributes to what manifests in my life—for good or for ill.

I knew my passion was suffocating at this job so, despite my fears, I began planning a "jailbreak." I went for job counseling, took personality tests, did informational interviews, and finally became willing to go to any lengths. "I know I'll get paid less for doing meaningful work, but being true to myself is more important than making good money," I said nobly. Talk about assumptions! Talk about a setup! Before I had a chance to quit, the office folded. I was given a generous severance package, and great God Almighty, I was free at last.

I spent the next four years at a variety of non-profit organizations, doing my part to save the world from this or that horror while living out my expectations of toiling long and hard for meager wages. I had difficulty pacing my passion and drive: I worked too much and too hard. I'd work and work and work until after a few months or weeks, even days, I'd collapse into devastating fatigue. At first I called this workaholism. Then I identified it as a form of unintentional self-abuse. Now I understand it as a form of debting—physical, emotional and spiritual debting. Whatever it was called, it brought me to my knees many times. Every time I fell I'd try to fix myself with dietary changes, exotic alternative healing, even plain old self-control. I'd recover for awhile, but ultimately resume my pattern.

My last job manifested my visions. I was in media; I was in the recovery field; and I was the boss. I felt so important, and my ego loved this job. But it was yet another struggling non-profit. I had more responsibility in this job than any before. I had a payroll to meet, a public to serve. More responsibility translated into more hours and more stress. Even when I wasn't technically on the job, it was with me inside. I went to bed making to-do notes and woke up with my mind running, planning, and mentally scheduling my day. At the same time, because my income was inadequate and I had no health insurance, some of my basic physical needs were not being met. I worked at that job for over two years, and my physical, emotional and spiritual health declined precipitously. Not only was I suffering crippling fatigue, I'd wake in the night with various parts of my body in spasms. My teeth were being worn down from unconscious grinding. During the last few months I had outbursts of screaming, sobbing and kicking walls in the office. But what does D.A. have to do with this?

During my tenure at the organization, I became close friends with two women whom I respected. Both were in D.A. I noticed they didn't talk much about money. They talked about moving out of scarcity and into abundance. I began to hear my story. In time, I went to my first D.A. meeting. D.A. has been my primary program ever since. I still didn't relate much to people who spoke about compulsive spending or racking up huge credit card debt: those weren't my issues. Instead, at least as many people were recovering from chronic deprivation, scarcity, underearning and various forms of self-debting. That was a revelation to me. The notion that you can debt yourself in all kinds of ways provided a new lens for viewing my chronic problems. Suddenly, I saw how not taking care of myself was a form of self-debting. I also began to see the many ways that I did not take care of myself: everything from not taking a nap when my body was pleading with me to forcing myself to swim when I was exhausted or not allowing myself enough time to get to an important appointment. These behaviors are forms of self-denial, denying the genuine needs of my body or spirit. Self-denial is ultimately self-debting: I am depleting my health account, say, or my pleasure account by not taking care of myself. Eventually the balance will come due.

I continued to work as a publisher while attending meetings regularly. I was blessed with Pressure Relief Groups that were more creative, inspiring and supportive than I knew possible. I took a variety of measures aimed at making my work situation healthy, like not working through lunch and hiring an administrative assistant, etc. I tried, friends, I really tried, because my ego was mightily attached to this job. It took some time to recognize that by feeding my ego, I was starving my soul and destroying my health. This was debting most profound.

In October 1989 came the great San Francisco earthquake. I was at the office, of course. Something in me shifted along with the tectonic plates, because after the quake I became willing to let go of my job. And so I began a process that would take over four months. I was terrified that I would not be able to take care of myself. When my Pressure Relief Group asked me what I wanted, I replied that I wanted to do nothing for six months. And I meant nothing. I was so rest-depleted that I knew I could not work—anywhere. And, being a chronic underearner, I had maybe one month's worth of living expenses as a "prudent reserve." I did not believe there was any way I could meet my needs without working.

My Pressure Relief Group, noting all the physical ailments I had as a result of the stress, including a shoulder injury from "Macintoshing" so hard, suggested that I might be eligible for disability benefits, even Workers Compensation. Disability?! I cried, I'm not disabled! Being a good New Ager, I was loathe to hang a label on myself. I feared that might lend energy to an unwanted diagnosis. But the truth is that I was disabled, a wreck. And I was so desperate and in such pain that I became willing to file a Workers Compensation claim. With that, I left my job. Miraculously, I was eligible to receive disability benefits—both for my shoulder injury and emotional stress. I had enough money to live on, and I proceeded to devote myself to napping, healing, getting massages and other health care treatments. I began to practice a fundamental tenet of D.A.: I was at last taking care of myself.

A funny thing happened on the way to my healing, something I didn't plan, ask for or have any idea I wanted. I became an artist. It started out innocently enough. I was expressing my pain and anguish with colored pencils. The results looked pretty much like a kindergartner's early crayon efforts. I didn't care. I was not an artist; this was just a therapeutic process—and a fine one, I might add. At some point, I looked at something I had drawn and said to myself: "Hey, this looks like art." Gradually, my work evolved to where I loved it as art. To my surprise, so did other people.

Meanwhile, poetry had begun to flow through me. This was as unexpected as discovering myself as an artist, because I'd always disliked poetry. Now, too, I was a poet. I was reading in public, and people were liking my stuff. Eventually, I would produce a book of poetry and art. The point here is that once I stopped debting myself and started to put my real needs first, I was given the greatest gift of all: my creativity. And, as a special bonus, I discovered that these forms of self-expression fed my soul, my spirit, and my ego. Who could ask for more? Well, me. I had yet to manifest financial abundance. I only made enough to get by.

I spent two glorious years on disability. I call this the best thing I ever did for myself, after getting clean and sober. When the benefits ended, I still felt unready to re-enter the work force. I needed more rest, I told my Pressure Relief Group. I needed more time to heal. My sponsor opined that if I wasn't ready to work, I didn't have to. I needed another miracle, and I got one. One of the D.A. principles I love is: *Ask for what you want.* I'm pretty good at that, getting better all the time. So out of a Pressure Relief Group came the idea: Advertise for an arts patron. Ask the universe very specifically for financial support and a free place to live while developing my work as an artist and producing a documentary on—surprise—workaholism.

My conscious intention, combined with material world advertising and the support of the Universe, created a five-bedroom family estate in a posh suburb of San Francisco—with a pool in the backyard and a laser printer in the study. I had my own wing, no less. My patron was a retired gentlemen who traveled often and wanted a human presence in the house. He also liked being a patron of the arts. He did not, however, give me any grant money. Believe me, from where I was coming, a free place to live—a beautiful, abundant, tree-, cricket- and deer-filled place to live—yes, a free place to live was plenty. I was in heaven. I spent nearly a year there, focusing on my art and poetry, producing my book. The documentary evolved instead to be a non-fiction book, which I began to write. I made a tremendous effort to create a desktop publishing business in hopes of making enough money to support myself working only part time, so I could work on my books, which would eventually generate abundant income. The business did not fulfill my vision, so I did temporary office work to meet my needs. After nearly a year in paradise, my patron decided to sell the house, so I had to leave. His parting gift to me was a requested $5,000 check for computer equipment of my own.

I moved in with my mother until I could find a permanent home and started working as a temp full time to make ends meet, since I was paying rent now. In this environment I began to experience the full impact of how so many of us live: doing work we don't like, working ourselves to a physical and emotional frazzle, having no time to nurture a spiritual life with little energy at the end of a day for anything more than dinner and TV. This was a nightmare existence for me. Fortunately, it was an opportunity to harvest abundant material for my book. All the while, I worked desperately to create another rent-free living situation. Then I checked in with myself. I've found my spirit speaks to me very directly through my body. So I asked: How is it that I want to provide for myself? The responding impulses surging up from my solar plexus roared: Get your own place! I said okay.

I'm understanding at even deeper levels how essential it is that I learn how to create abundant income for myself, so that I no longer need to rely on windfalls, gifts or kindness of strangers. I am committed to learning how to take care of myself on all levels at the same time. For example, having a lavishly paid job that numbs the soul won't work. Nor will an emotionally and spiritually satisfying job that pays slave wages. Nor will any work that takes up so much of my life that I don't have time for friends, leisure, play, reflection, or travel. Taking care of myself is a tall order. I have few models for a fully self-loving life. And this is my path. I give thanks that I have D.A. to support me on this path. I am grateful to be part of this mutually supportive community of people committed to their visions. D.A. has expanded my belief in what's possible, encouraged me to go for my vision, and erased my willingness to "settle." I have faith that with continued commitment to the D.A. principles that are true for me, my gratitude and loving partnership with the Universal Life Spirit, and my willingness to grow and change, I will complete the creation of my vision: a life where I am happy, successful, prosperous and of service, doing what I love to do.

The Slow Burn Pauper
Becomes the Soaring Visionary

*This debtor found deep support through fellowship
and active participation in the program.*

If you put a frog in a pan of water and slowly heat the water to boiling, the frog won't move. It stays in the boiling water until it dies. But if you poke the frog, it will jump out. This is a metaphor for my life.

With vagueness, low-grade depression, and a passionless life, I was like the frog in boiling water. I was not jumping out but slowly dying, not having the energy to jump. I was not even aware of the seriousness of my problem. I was running on empty, quitting when things got too painful and never succeeding at anything I cared about. That was how I lived my life before coming to D.A.

I came into D.A. with no income, getting by month to month, slowly sinking into debt year after year for over a decade. I was a pauper and self-debtor, chronically underearning. I was always fatigued and had a low-grade depression. I didn't have a vision or hope for the future, just a fantasy that one day my ship would come in and "the big bucks fix" would make my life work. Also, I was dependent upon occasional loans and gifts from my parents to bail me out and get by. I never had a job I was committed to or cared about. I was divorced and a pauper with poor self-esteem.

I made investments that failed. I took a job that literally didn't pay anything. (It was commission only, and I never made a commission). I never bought new clothes. My credit cards were my emergency fund for vacations or classes. I would borrow money with good intentions to pay it back, but never had the resources to do so.

I had a good education, a good family, but my life went nowhere. I lived a "wannabe" existence, without motivation to follow through the actions to succeed. The pain of the worst relationship of my life, a relationship that heightened my codependency and accentuated my compulsive debting disease, brought me to my knees. It was then that I walked into my first D.A. meeting.

When I entered these rooms four and a half years ago, my life began to change. It has been better every day since. I remember what the newcomers leader said. "This disease will kill you. It will send you to prison, or bring you to commit suicide." I knew I was dying. I saw for the first time that my life was slowly wasting away. From that day forward, I have taken my program deadly seriously. I have consistently worked the Steps, called my sponsor, made outreach and bookend calls, given service, and had Pressure Relief Groups. It is a simple program, but it hasn't been easy. Fear and familiar defenses were all there to stop me, but my Higher Power and my new D.A. family were all there to get me through.

There is an incredible miracle going on in my life, inside and out. "Visions" is what I like to call Phase Two D.A. About two and a half years into the program, I heard about the idea of opening up to what I really wanted in my life. I had a Pressure Relief Group for the purpose of listing everything I wanted to be, do, or have. We met for over five hours, and I hear that some sessions have even gone longer. For each item on my list, I was told to "research and pray." This model has brought amazing abundance into my life.

I had a vision of my Southwest dream home. For three months after that initial visions Pressure Relief Group, I did footwork. My real estate agent, a D.A. member, and I were out horseback riding in the area that interested me. There was a Southwest house with French doors and fireplace, as if it had been dropped from a spaceship. And it was for sale! Being the good debtor I was, I had no income or savings. I went to my parents to borrow the down payment to be secured against the house and found a one-hundred-thousand dollar inheritance from my grandfather that could only be used towards purchasing a home. I had prayed for exactly that amount!

Next in miracleland, the property was in foreclosure. I was able to ride through all the ups and downs of purchasing this property with the support of D.A. and my newfound self-esteem. At the end, the deal died. But God, in the form of the seller's mortgage insurance company, stepped in and resurrected it. We were finally able to close escrow, and I moved into my new home. Knowing I was a chronic underearner, I asked in my original vision that the property be self-supporting. Lo and behold, I had become a landlord to two tenants who rented the other two houses on my property.

Another one of my visions was to have a horse. I had no idea how this was going to happen. I lived on horse property, so I built a corral. I went with the theory, "Build it, and they will come." And they did—not one, but two horses!

Eleven months after that visions Pressure Relief Group, I was living in that house, with the French doors and fireplace. Six months later, I had Mouse, my horse, who went with it. I went from renting a one-room apartment in a low-rent area, barely able to pay the electricity bill, to owning my own Southwest dream home, which I call the "Adobe Dream." Getting the Adobe Dream is a D.A. miracle.

In my third year I started a visions meeting. Six of us met once a week. Now, a year and a half later, it's an eager group of fifteen, each of us opening our lives to our visions, as we opened our lives to one another regarding our debting. It's amazing how each person seems to catch the wave of the visions and be off and running to incredible new adventures. Some of the alumni are in other parts of the country and the world, living the visions they unveiled in our meeting.

My biggest vision is still way way beyond my current belief systems (just like the house, the horse and the car...). It is to own my own Learjet! I surrender the results to God, stick with what got me here, "research and pray," and one day look forward to telling you about that miracle.

I have worked my program as if my life depended on it, and it does. I have a sponsor. I work the Steps. I go to meetings. I use the phone to bookend. But the real key to my recovery is my service: secretary, newcomers leader, treasurer, GSR (General Service Representative) to two World Conferences, and weekly Pressure Relief Group commitments for others. That keeps me coming back and focused on my recovery. There are still many days that I don't feel like showing up, but because of my D.A. habit, service, you know where I will be on a Tuesday night.

I feel the gifts of D.A. are threefold. First, I stopped the debting cycle and gained the esteem of taking responsibility for my own life. Second, I built a community of support and friendship, so that I will not be alone. Third, I had a spiritual awakening, a renewed gratitude, and a communion with my Higher Power out of the ashes of my dysfunction and depression. Oh, and four, I opened up to a belief in visions and passions that has transformed the physical, mental, emotional, social, and spiritual areas of my life in magnitude.

Recently, we were all in a California earthquake. Immediately following, D.A. members who had lost their apartments came to at my door and found a place to stay through our network. Many offered their homes and any help that was needed. A group of us went to help pick up at a friend's apartment. On the second evening, a group of us were at my house and shared our common experience and feelings. We had a camping meal with no light, gas or running water, and I felt the greatest bond of fellowship, love, and caring any person could have. We all checked in with each other and with any needs we had. I received calls from fellow D.A.s from around the country who spent days trying to get through to my phone.

Being a debtor has been an incredible gift in my life. On the practical side, I have reduced my debt by half in four and a half years. My net worth has grown to over a quarter of a million dollars. I doubled my income last year and hope to do it again this year, which is another visions stretch beyond my belief, but it is in God's hands.

I still sometimes cannot pay my bills in a timely manner. The difference today is that I no longer feel like a victim. I take reality on its own terms, negotiating with my creditors and making payments I can afford after taking care of myself first. I am pursuing one of my visions, writing, by meeting in a weekly writing group of D.A.s. I have a career job in the field of my dreams and an unlimited potential for income based on my ability and willingness to take action, something D.A. has taught me.

It used to be beyond my belief that I would ever be able to get past my disease. I couldn't see my way out. I had been in therapy for years. I had done all the self-help workshops. I had a desire to succeed, but my dysfunction, pain, and fear were stronger. Only through D.A. did I find strong enough recovery to begin to live the life I truly wanted. It is one day at a time. Often my fear is great, but it no longer immobilizes me. If my life is as astoundingly different four years from now as it is from four years ago, I won't recognize my former self!

My Surrender to D.A.

This debtor needed a lot of courage to face her creditors. She found it with the help of her Pressure Relief Group.

When I first came to D.A. I was like a hamster or gerbil on a treadmill. I was racing faster and faster, working harder and harder to try to improve my situation, but it stayed the same no matter what I did. There was never enough money.

I paid all my bills late. I couldn't bring my credit card balances down. I owed $50,000 to my lawyer for a very nasty divorce, and I was constantly using my credit line. I alternated between spending as little as possible in an attempt to manage things and periodically spending when I couldn't stand the deprivation any longer. I overworked six or seven days a week, often evenings.

One year before I came to my first D.A. meeting, I had resolved to make more money. Surely that would be the answer to my financial problems. I was successful in increasing my income by a significant amount, but my situation remained exactly the same. I was baffled. I had tried everything I could think of; finally, I gave up. A friend had been telling me about D.A. for years, so I decided to give it a try.

What I heard at my first few meetings gave me hope. Since all my efforts had failed, I resolved to do whatever these D.A. people told me to do. I began by writing down everything I spent, getting rid of my credit cards, and paying my bills on time. After some initial shyness, I began talking to people after meetings, getting their phone numbers and calling them.

I knew I needed to stop all forms of debting, that I needed to not incur any new unsecured debt. I was still involved in a custody battle with my ex-husband. I realized that continuing to use my lawyer's services would be debting, unless I paid her for those services promptly and in full. It was frightening to let go of her services in the middle of the custody case. As I shared this in a meeting, expressing all my fear and uncertainty, I cried. I said I needed a Pressure Relief Meeting. What an outpouring of support I received, including a woman who agreed to be on my Pressure Relief Group. I was so grateful.

Finding a man for my first Pressure Relief Group was harder. I asked men at every meeting I went to, but none were available. Finally, one Saturday morning, I called someone in D.A. who suggested I go to every meeting I could possibly get to—several each day if necessary—and ask every appropriate man. I took his advice and went to a meeting that afternoon. I heard a man with an inspiring qualification and promptly asked him to be my pressure man. Much to my surprise and joy, he said yes.

The love, support, and relief I felt from that first Pressure Relief Meeting was powerful. When they suggested that I take a moratorium on my debt payments, I was shocked. I left the meeting convinced that I would not have the courage to do such a thing. About a week later I decided to do what my Pressure Relief Group had suggested. I knew this meant giving up my lawyer. She would not represent me unless I continued to pay her $100 each week against my debt to her.

I contacted all of my creditors, both by phone and in writing. I kept a record of all calls and copies of all correspondence. I made lots of D.A. bookending calls before and after contacting my creditors. I called my lawyer to let her know I would not be able to pay her for a while. She was furious and accused me of destroying her law practice. I was shaking, in a cold sweat. My heart was pounding, but because my pressure people had given me a script to follow and coached me, my voice was calm. I stuck to my script and didn't engage in any argument. I always assured all my creditors of my commitment to pay them the money I owed.

I began to take action toward finding affordable legal help. This was an act of faith. I made numerous phone calls and followed every lead. In the end I was offered free legal help from two sources. This was a D.A. miracle to me—just one of the many proofs I've experienced that I do have a Higher Power looking out for me. When I am committed to not debting, my Higher Power provides whatever I need.

Is it Time for Me Yet?

*This member unknotted a tangle of personal threads
to create a colorful fabric.*

My greatest fear is that my life would pass unlived. It seemed to me as a child that the adults around me were only half alive. They seemed to be used up and so absorbed in the daily routines of work, housework, and child rearing that they never got around to living personal dreams. I was a child of the Sixties. The sky was the limit: We were going to remake the world, people were going to wake up, or the world was going to end in nuclear war, greed, and pollution. My parents were children of the Great Depression of the Thirties. Their dreams of financial prosperity, a beautiful home, and college for all their kids seemed like dreaming about what I expected as a God-given right, not something to base a life on. To me, life seemed to be a choice between conforming and being commonplace for financial well-being and lackluster spirit, or living out your ideals and spiritual values that made you poor, but happy.

I chose then to be poor, but "fully alive." It wasn't until I began my recovery in Debtors Anonymous that I saw that being financially prosperous was not a moral issue.

I was the oldest child in an alcoholic, compulsively overeating family. As the oldest daughter, I was my mother's assistant in taking care of three other children and my needy and demanding alcoholic father. I never saw my mother read a book or have a hobby or speak of any dreams other than dreams for her children. In other words, I saw my mother living only for us, not for herself. I knew I did not want to be like her. But I did not see how to be different, and I was attracted to her spiritual, selfless, and loving nature.

My father, on the other hand, was a powerful executive in a big corporation. For his daily sacrifice at the office, he spent his time catering completely to his desires to relax, read, fish, swim, and watch television, all while drinking to unwind. I knew I didn't want to be like him either, but his power and activities were a lot more attractive to me than housework.

Unfortunately, I drew certain conclusions from my family that eventually brought me to D.A.: Women work constantly, their reward is love and financial dependence, and the family suffers if they have other interests. As independent people, they simply don't count. Since women don't earn money out in the world, they must give all of their time to earn the financial and loving support of a man.

Now in my forties, I see that my mother chose and enjoyed her life, my father suffered from alcoholism and my mother from her codependency. I can see cultural biases that led me to these horrible conclusions. The evidence is abundant that women have not been valued in the workplace as highly as men. The irony for me is that I set out to value myself, live my life fully, and be second to no man in relationship, but I have still found myself living out the old script. I carry within me a disease that sabotages and squanders all my resources: money, time, love, and energy.

My nightmare is that I will wake up one day and the great proctor of life will say, "Close your test booklet. Put your pencil down. Your time is up."

How has my time debting affected my life? In short, I have lost years of my life in addictive relationships. Twice I have almost destroyed my precious body by overworking. Underearning is another form of time debting that has profoundly affected my sense of self and my ability to take care of myself. Dreams have flown out the window while I was busy doing what I thought I had to do before I could get to myself. I never let myself envision many dreams, because what was the point? I'd never be able to make them come true.

The healing process has been gradual. I have been learning to live life one day at a time through practicing the Twelve Steps. I came into recovery from codependency in Al-Anon four years before I entered Debtors Anonymous. I had to stop my addiction to people before I could even know that my life was my own. My body, my time, my work, and my love all belong to me. It has been revolutionary to live my life when I really believe that.

Al-Anon gave me my life back, but Debtors Anonymous taught me how to live for myself. I came into D.A. with few financial debts, but I suffered from a severe intestinal disorder caused by overwork. I had compulsively used up my life energy. I was on empty, thoroughly exhausted, and had diarrhea for over a year.

My company's disability payments were higher than my salary had been before, but I lived in terror that there was no room for me on this planet, no time for me to heal, and I was unable to work. I was face to face with my belief that my value was only in what I could do or be for someone else. D.A. and my loving Higher Power helped me know I am a sweet and precious woman, no matter what I do or do not do. I am worthy of great love and all of life's bounty.

My D.A. sponsor insisted that my first job in D.A. recovery was to heal physically and emotionally. Much to my irritation, he insisted that I have lots of fun and entertainment. He suggested that I needed to learn to enjoy life and give myself pleasure. I thought he was a bit nuts! But I had done so much healing working the Twelve Steps in my other program that I gave him a chance. Next came his insistence that I had deprived myself of a relationship. Since recovery, I had met my emotional needs with friendships, and the thought of a relationship struck terror into my heart. But I slowly opened my mind to the idea that having a relationship would be part of a full life. One day at a time, I learned there was enough time for me, enough money, enough love. The fear that I had to sacrifice myself in either love or work left me.

A relationship bloomed in my life with a fellow member of D.A. We have enjoyed the gifts of recovery in our love. We have weathered the challenges of learning to be two complete people while in a relationship for almost six years. I have not been absorbed, destroyed or felt second-class. I have felt the old pull to postpone my dreams until the laundry is done. The old script of "I come later" is still present, but our relationship and recovery seldom support it.

Pressure Relief Groups have been invaluable in supporting me in learning how to have, claim and work toward my visions in a solvent way. In the past two years, I have had the joy of visions coming true. My partner and I have moved from the city to a farm, and we feel we wake up every day in paradise. I have led groups of women on night hikes and experienced joy in seeing women claim their power walking fearlessly in the night. Both these visions were supported step by step by my Pressure Relief Groups, people in the program, and my Business Owners D.A. (BODA) meeting. Both these visions had seemed impossible before.

Recovery has been a process of understanding and accepting how life works. My original misconceptions about time, energy, and money brought me to my knees. My first challenge was to accept that I am an ordinary human being with physical needs and limitations. For a long time, the desire to transcend my body without accepting it was strong. For a long time, my physical illness brought me shame.

My magical thinking about time was very strong. I believed I could accomplish long daily "to do" lists, still having time to play and rest. Only daily work with my sponsor broke that spell. He kept saying a full life meant balance, not accomplishing huge numbers of important things. So every day, I went over my "to do" list with him. There could be no more than ten items, balanced between spiritual, business, fun, and home.

Growing a vegetable garden on our farm taught me about the true nature of time. In magic time, I plant and harvest on the same day. In my garden, I learned that making the way clear and preparing the soil takes time. Composting is like the inner work of recovery that transforms garbage into rich soil. Envisioning and planning the garden must come before the seeds are planted. Many seeds must be planted, as not every plant will flourish. There are many days of watering, weeding and protecting new seedlings, or ideas, before they become established. For a long time the ground stays barren, and we can't see if anything has sprouted.

Then it seems like the work is futile when gophers and insects devour some of the plants. Obstacles rise to block my visions, and I think I have to give up my dreams. By starting small and protecting the vision, I allow my life and my garden to unfold in their own way and time. Eventually, it's time to harvest and bring in all the bounty.

Harvesting my life is when I enjoy and share my abundance. Then it's time to feed the soil again and dream new dreams. Being present is the key to living abundantly. Realizing that I am part of a Power greater than myself and that this Higher Power is in charge of time has allowed me to relax and trust. When I ask my Higher Self what is the best use of my time now, I feel peaceful and able to meet whatever is next.

As a compulsive pauper, I have been able to keep a lot of money out of my life. Time, however, must be spent some way, and we all have twenty-four hours a day. As a time debtor, I was lost in the swirl of compulsively spending away life. I wasn't only late for appointments; I was late for my life.

Now, living in the present, I feel the birth of the future. Accepting my humanity and my limitations, I spend less energy fighting life. The more I heal, the more I value myself and my visions. The more I live in balance one day at a time, the more energy I have for creativity. Believing that my visions are a gift from my Higher Power, I realize a Power greater than myself wants me to live and share abundantly. The world is no longer powerful enough to stop me when I rest in God's will.

I am poised on the edge of a great leap forward into my Greater Self. Embracing myself and all my pain, I turn my will and my life over to my Higher Power.

Dream of Peace

D.A. became an invaluable source in her developing spirituality.

I was born in the Middle East. My dad was frugal and pretty much sick about money. My mom had an "abundance consciousness" and a generosity that flipped, however, into compulsive spending. My country was not very materialistic at the time, yet my parents' patterns and behavior created a lot of stress at home, and all of it was money-related.

As a little girl that wanted to keep her parents together, I decided to reduce the stress and not "want" anything from my parents. Needless to say, this kept me isolated from children's activities that involved money. I lied, saying that I didn't like ice cream, that I didn't really feel like taking a ride on a boat, that I couldn't go out because my mother expected me early, even that I couldn't tolerate the idea of summer camp, and on and on.

I didn't go to many birthday parties, because I wanted to avoid asking my parents to buy a gift. However, I was brave enough once and did ask. My dad gave me a fancy pen for the birthday girl. When my friend opened the gifts, she made fun of my present in front of everyone, because etched on the other side of the pen was my father's office name and address.

The hardest part of our deprivation was my father trying to cut utility bills by washing me in cold water, though we were never poor, nor did we lack money to meet any basic needs.

Through the years, the isolation became worse. I was a bright kid with no desire to study, even though I was in a special art school. I was afraid that if I studied, everyone might find out I wasn't as smart as they thought. Education is highly valued in my homeland, and being a bad student threw me out of the "in" circle. I started to develop an image as "different" which I'm grateful for today, because it gave me the strength to do things that took guts, going where no one else had been before.

At 18, I joined the army. Serving was a familiar concept, because all of our life, we knew one day we would be called for duty. My army service was unexpectedly functional. My deep love for the land and the people put me in a realm where I could see and act clearly. Inside, however, my spirit was devastated because it was crystal clear now that I wanted to be "wheat in a storm," one that moves with the wind. Like a leaf on a green tree, I wanted to be an integral part of nature, yet I felt contaminated. Nature was pure and light, and I was heavy.

After two and a half years, I finished my service holding in my hand a half a year's salary. The reality was harsh. I had no motivation, no emotional capability to be productive. I felt paralyzed and didn't know how to pull myself out. I found it hard to rise above living in a tribal family in a troubled country. I needed perspective, a breathing space. Just before, my parents had gone to Europe and left me a business space to use as a children's summer camp. It was an easy job with short hours, and I made a lot of money which I spent on cabs, restaurants, and friends. When the job was over, I knew I had to leave the country. I didn't understand why; I just knew it had to do with my survival.

I made plans to go abroad and was shocked to find that I had $200 left from my "big money-making job." I couldn't understand where all the money went. Right there, I made an unconscious promise to myself to be like my father, which meant holding on to every penny.

My mother convinced me to go to America where we had relatives, instead of Europe. She said she'd pay for my ticket if I'd go to America and not Europe. I agreed. With $200, and $600 that my dad surprised me with at the last minute, hardly any English, and a desire to stay alive, I got myself on an airplane headed to where the sidewalks, so they said, were made of gold.

My first time in New York City could be a story by itself.

I moved many times that first year, living in crazy apartments with crazy people. My American relatives offered money as a gift, but I refused. I was too proud, and I had to maintain my state of deprivation. The biggest struggle during my first year in America was to stay sane. Many times I thought I would lose it.

I worked as much as possible, but none of my jobs used my natural skills, so I gained no self-esteem. It never occurred to me to look for a job that was my heart's desire, even when I learned English and got my permanent resident status.

A friend of mine dragged me to Al-Anon. This began my spiritual path. I heard a woman mention Debtors Anonymous in a meeting. She told me where to find meetings and mentioned the terms "underearner" and "deprivation" as if they never existed before in English. My first Debtors Anonymous meeting was shocking. I think I was shocked to find out that others also carry this most embarrassing obsession of all.

I remember my mother telling how my father would sit in a dark bathroom to save electricity, how he ate foods with mold, how whenever there was free food my father would pile on an amount that would compete with an elephant, and how he would steal razor blades from supermarkets in foreign countries, all while he was a diplomat for our country. In the end, my mom always added how grateful she was that she could tell this to me because, God forbid, how could she possibly tell this to any other living soul?

At the end of the first meeting, it was not pretty to discover that I had taken after my dad, that I suffered from the same horrible deprivation monster that came into my family, probably many generations ago. I wanted to get myself out of this private prison, and the only thing I knew was to go to meetings. "It works if you work it!" was not a joke for me. I took it seriously and used every possible tool. I went to at least seven meetings a week. After three months, I began to lead a beginners' record-keeping meeting. Although this part of the program was difficult for many, I liked it because I discovered I had a good memory for numbers. I remembered how much I spent during the day, down to the exact penny. For the first time, my obsession with figures took a positive turn.

Next was the Pressure Relief Group. At that time, D.A. was eight years old. While only a few people were old timers, many newcomers knocked at their door for a Pressure Relief Group. I had to wait in line for this important salvation day. In the meantime, I used other tools. It was clear that D.A. was not a "talk" program. D.A. was totally-action oriented. If I wished to work the program, I might find myself doing a thing or two I didn't expect, even in my wildest dreams. The energy in the rooms was so uplifting that I was proud to belong. It felt like a winner's program. For someone who hated every person that carried a briefcase, it was a strong healing experience in "equality" to be in the same room with famous artists, heads of companies, sharp lawyers, or other underearners, underachievers like myself. Tools, like the business meetings, helped, as well as the fact that I learned the format business people used. Now I no longer felt like an ignorant baby shuffled around by a bunch of briefcases.

Another profound healing experience was men sharing their incest stories; how incest set up their feelings of worthlessness, deprivation and low self-esteem, resulting in debting. I too had incest issues to resolve. I had never known that men were victims of sexual abuse and also shed tears, especially the ones with the briefcases.

At my second or third Pressure Relief Group, a "big one" was dropped on me. Close to Christmas, they asked me what I would do when my school closed for a month. "I can be a bicycle messenger," I replied without hesitation. I heard, "Is this all you know or can do? Your gifts are in the arts. What is this about a bicycle messenger?" Then they gave me an action, to buy *The Village Voice* every week and mark all the job offers that were art-related. They were strict about my not making any phone calls or doing interviews. "Just mark down the ads!" they said. Well, I did it. I thought it was a brilliant action, because in a most simple way, I got exactly what I needed. Through the ads I learned there is life up from Greenwich Village, and that this life was inviting. In three weeks, I was employed in a printmaking studio with a wonderful, loving environment. The job didn't come through the ads, but my awareness opened a space for it, and through friends, it fell into my lap.

I went to at least two visions meetings a week and understood that without a vision, my "walk" doesn't have a direction. One of the people who inspired me was a fifty-year-old architect, who decided to pursue his vision to host a talk show. Within three months, he managed to become host of his favorite talk show. I said to myself, "If he can do it with the responsibility of a wife, children, house and a car, I can do it too." I put out in my Pressure Relief Group that I would like to do window displays.

It seems that three is a magic number in the program. Within three weeks, I was on the display team that worked in highly exclusive stores in the Fifty-Seventh Street and Fifth Avenue area. How did I do it? Simple: The D.A. way! Little actions bring great results. Coming back from the Pressure Relief Group, I wrote on my calendar every other day "D.A. action." On those days, I had to speak at least once with someone in the design field. On the other days, I asked people if they knew anybody in this field. On "D.A. action" day, I made only one phone call to people I knew. Shortly, I ran out of names, so the next thing was to call people I'd met two, three, or five years ago, maybe at a party or other social event. This action brought great discomfort, especially embarrassment, but I did it anyway. I thought, what do I have to lose? I found that people are usually happy to help.

Doing displays was like playing. For the first time ever, I earned my living from something I loved doing. My self-esteem meter jumped way up, and now it was time for a new realization. I did love the display job. Yet I was still under-earning, making no more than $10 an hour. My pressure people showed me that to follow my vision list, I needed to start at $25 an hour and work my way to $65. The next day, I showed up at the printing studio and asked for $25 an hour. My boss-partner was making $12. The person that hired us told me it was impossible, so I left the job. The printing was most of my income, but I had to trust and open a space for abundance. That was one of the scariest things I have ever done; it had to be that way. Again, I made an agreement with God, or the way I refer to God now, the Great Mystery, that this "standing in truth" would not cost me debt. After a week, the head of my studio called and said she had found a way for me to get $25 an hour. She connected me with two artists; I gained two jobs where I designed my own hours and would work at home.

With gratitude I put my heart and my soul into the prints. I meditated on them, talked to them and filled them up with the energy of love. They sold with the speed of light. After a while, one of the artists told me I was too expensive, and he could hire me only when he needed a spotless job. I understood, but told him I couldn't take my fee down because it would hurt my self-esteem.

Life was shaping up. The program was an important spiritual foundation, and now I wanted to expand on it. I had enough money for workshops and lectures given by spiritual teachers and masters. One of these teachers gave a meditation one day and asked us to visualize a place where we felt really safe. In my mind's eye came a Yoga center where a friend of mine spent her summer. The lecture went on, sharing how we listen to God twenty-four hours a day. That was a puzzling idea for me. A month later, no free-lance job was to be found anywhere. At that time, I was rooted in D.A. principles and knew if I made a constant effort and no work came through, God probably wanted me to do something else. I said, "Okay God, I don't know how to listen to You, but I'm sure going to find out." I stayed in my room for two weeks, mostly trying to grasp what God was telling me. In my mind's eye, I kept getting a flash of the Yoga center from my meditation. So, my thick big head finally got it! I was stripped of jobs and a relationship, free to go to the Yoga center, something I probably would not have done under any other circumstances. I had a week to wrap up my life in New York City in order to get to the next training. The sublet arrived at the last minute. After all the expenses were paid, I was left with $67.

I know that spirituality is my main focus, and my vision is to be a spiritual teacher. The Yoga center was an important imprint on my life. The guru there recommended not to jump from one thing to the another, but to "Choose one path and go as deep as you can." That felt like truth. I had to make a choice. I loved the Yoga center, yet my heart was with the Native American philosophy because that fulfilled my old desire of being integrated with nature. When I did make my choice, the "hole" that was pounding that "something is missing," the emptiness, filled quietly.

I spent four and a half years on a Native American reservation, living by D.A. principles. Although I was too far away from any D.A. meetings, I kept records. I was the only one with a car, job and no debts among our permanent residents. When I first came, there was absolutely nothing. With my education for abundance, I set up a foundation for an office with fancy equipment and people to run it, all without debting. I started with the "office space" by raffling a picture that someone donated, and I continued to build, looking only for projects that could pay for themselves.

Today, I'm in transition, getting prepared to go back to my homeland. I lived with this particular Native American nation because they were part of a Peace Confederacy of five nations that had lived in peace for hundreds of years. Coming from a troubled land, I was willing to cope with discomfort in order to learn the principles of peace that held this Confederation together. The form of my vision was to bring peace back with me to the Middle East. I put all the little pleasures that make life worth living on hold to focus my intense study on fulfilling my mission.

Recently, after taking another Native elder to teach in my country, I had a major revelation that brought me grief and disappointment. I discovered I'm only human. Although I wanted perfect harmony with the Earth like the animals and birds, eagles are eagles and people are people. I might be a peacemaker, but my primary responsibility is to enjoy every moment, right here, right now. A teacher once said that living in the future or the past is to deny God, because good is present right now.

After years of spiritual training and teaching principles of spirituality. I found that most important for me is to enjoy the scent of a flower, the touch of the wind, always remembering to give thanks to the sun for light and warmth, to the Earth for food, to the moon that measures time, and to the precious breath of life. It has been said: Thank you Great Mystery.

From Resentment to Freedom

Lateness became an antidote for being the lost child in my family.

Today I'm living in a miracle. I've been in the D.A. program for a year and a half, and I can definitely say I've grown in ways I could have never predicted. I was born to a family in Texas, to people who never grew up enough to realize their dreams. My mother got married because she was pregnant with me, and my father took care of her when she dropped out of school to have me. She never experienced life on her own. My father never really grew up either. He drank every day and gave up law school to work for his father in the family business. Even now, they are still dependent and resentful of my grandparents, who support them. In my family, the grandparents are the moneybags who dole it out or hang on to it when they want. They are the adults and my fortyish parents are the children.

This is my background, and I thank God and D.A. for showing me a way to support myself and be my own person financially and emotionally. As I drove home from my D.A. meeting, I thought to myself that I could write a how-to manual for people raised to be dependent. There are probably a lot of us out there. When I got a car, I went to full service because I didn't know how to pump gas. When I entered college, I didn't know how to put in a load of laundry. I can see why, because my parents did everything for me, without teaching me. I learned to look for others to take care of me, believing somehow it would all work out. As I got older it translated to "The money will be there." As I got even older, I realized my father was totally vague about money. In a sense he "borrowed" money from bills to buy presents or extravagant vacations. To this day, my parents' money is play money. All the real stuff like house payments and children's education is handled by my grandparents. And my parents feel that is their right. They are actually resentful of my grandparents' money, feeling they should have more.

I learned this resentment. In fact, I've felt rage and resentment since I was young. When I was a child, every morning I would wait until my mother called and called me to breakfast before I would move a muscle to get dressed. Every day I would be in trouble. Often my father would yell at me all the way to school about how lazy I was for being late. One day, my father dropped me off at school fifteen minutes late, and I walked into the first grade classroom to find no one there. I was terrified. All the lights were off. Screaming, I ran out to my dad's car, but he was already driving away. I ran after the car, fell and scraped my leg horribly. As it turned out, the school had had a fire drill. That is one of my earliest memories, and the trauma of lateness has always plagued me.

My family, friendships, relationships, every job I've had, every class I've taken, and everyone else I've known, without exception, have been affected by my being late. When I was five, my brother was born with a birth defect, requiring special attention from my parents. No longer the only child, my mother admitted I was ignored after his birth. My mother says she was a child herself. At the time she thought I was a big kid and could take care of myself. One of the most significant ways I acted out my childhood anger was by being late. Until I went away to college, my parents would call me, threaten to leave, and even drive off, leaving me in a panic. Occasionally they would hit me for holding things up. My lateness kept me from being invisible, my antidote for being the lost child in my family.

Growing up, I resented my father's temper and drinking. As a child, I was insatiable; you couldn't give me enough. What I really wanted was adults who would listen and acknowledge me, not merely buy something to make my pain go away. In high school, I attempted to impress my friends with expensive gifts from my large allowance. I would treat everyone to frozen yogurt after school; I drove a nice car. But I still thought I didn't have enough. I regularly stole money from my dad's wallet, a twenty here and a twenty there. I used my mother's credit cards to mail order things without asking. When they arrived, my mother was vague, and she didn't remember if she'd ordered them. I was in pain, dating to get out of the house, getting speeding tickets, zeros at school, and wrecking my car once a year. It was a painful existence.

My lateness, or time debting, became an ugly pattern in my relationships. My friends threatened to leave when I wasn't ready. At school, I would come to class late eating a doughnut. Who needed the student council? Lateness gave me all the notoriety a person could want. When I went away to college, I continued my tradition by showing up for class twenty minutes late. I could often be seen running with my class papers just as the professor was pulling out of the parking lot. Even the classes I took were determined by who would accept late papers.

In college, I was angry because I had the same allowance as in high school. I made up excuses to get more money. I would buy all kinds of books that weren't on the class list, Christmas presents, and food at the student store to get reimbursed. I would smile and think, "I made fifty dollars on that deal. Pretty good." Even though I was away from home, there was scarcity everywhere. In my family, the motto seemed to be "Get it while the getting's good." In this spirit, I hoarded things and food and spent money like crazy. Conveniently, my uncle worked in the bank where my checking account was, so he would bail me out every time I bounced a check. There were a lot of them! Or, my dad or my grandmother would bail me out. I never experienced paying the late fee, a real disservice to me, because if I had learned my lesson on my own, it wouldn't have happened often.

At one point, my dad gave me $500 for my photography class. Now that was a lot of money, and the equipment was expensive. But I thought to myself, I'm rich, I'm wealthy. I proceeded to buy myself all kinds of things. Guess what, it added up so there wasn't enough left for the photography equipment. And I bounced more checks. The idea was that you were supposed to spend the money real quick while it was there.

I eventually learned to handle my spending and supplemented my income with jobs. From time to time I would have episodes of vagueness, and my grandmother would bail me out. I got those student credit cards and the accompanying student debt. Even though I grew and learned about being independent and supporting myself, it was theoretical. No one told me what it would be like when I graduated: scary, lonely, and depressing. I remained blissfully ignorant and made no plans, but still graduated. For a few weeks, I fantasized that the world would offer me jobs right and left, but I had a problem: I wouldn't apply for jobs or graduate school, because I was afraid of rejection. Paralyzed with fear, I wanted someone to take care of me. Three months after graduation I lived in complete deprivation on a little money from my family and working twenty hours a week, providing only room and board. To my family, it was time to come back to the fold; the experiment was over. But the last thing I wanted was to leave where I was.

I lived in fear for many months. Was I just biding my time until an inevitable return in defeat? During those months of unhappiness, despair, and restlessness, I discovered I needed two things: recovery for money issues and recovery to deal with sexual and emotional abuse. I mention these together because my family background is related with my spending and attitude about money. When I am home with people who do not affirm or hear me, I become vulnerable to compulsive spending. I spend to impress them and to numb my pain.

People in my family used money as power over others. Today I know I do not have to tolerate abusive treatment in exchange for money. As my financial independence becomes reality, I have confidence that can protect me from dependent situations with family or otherwise.

A painful thing I've learned about lateness is that it's based on the belief that there is not enough time, in direct opposition to a D.A. affirmation. For me this belief came from not having enough time with my mother. In my family, money, time and affection were so scarce that we felt like we had to steal it. Time I stole by being late felt like my only free and peaceful moments, but this was passive-aggressive because of anger and resentment. I learned there is a relationship between my lateness and my resentment. If I am angry or upset or something is unresolved, I run late. If I feel honored and respected, I am accountable. Time debting does not work for me in the real world now. After struggling for so long, I am learning there is enough time to find what I need and enough time to enjoy myself. When I catch myself thinking there isn't enough money, love or time, I remember there is abundance in the world.

Running behind schedule also contributes to low self-esteem. Like an addict, I'm always running to catch up. Replaying old family scenes hoping to achieve different results is the definition of insanity. Instead of using my lateness as a test for unconditional love, I need to work the Steps on it: admitting my powerlessness, taking an inventory, and when I become ready, asking God to remove my character defects. Then I can move on to other lessons.

Now I have been in recovery for four years. I first went to D.A. in '92, and for the first few months, I just listened. People sounded hopeful. Like me, some were unemployed. Some were underemployed. Some were happy. A new experience for me, and a little strange. Wasn't life and work supposed to be drudgery? The meeting I chose as a home meeting covered everything: a speaker sharing experience, strength and hope, business, time debting and visions. Like time debting, the concept of visions piqued my interest: People can actually choose what they want in their lives and move toward their goals.

So I began to record my expenses in a nice, official-looking book, and I still have it. I also had my first Pressure Relief Group meeting. I highly recommend them. Talking to two people in the program about money and life issues is the most valuable tool of my Twelve Step program. It's nurturing that many of us didn't get. It's the practical information that people who were raised to be dependent didn't get. And some incredible miracles and growth are in there somewhere too. In my Pressure Relief Group, all three of us became good friends. The people in my group have the same issues I do, and they understand me. They accept me as I am, even my lateness. Being loved by these people has made a profound difference in my life, and I think in theirs too.

I have found myself volunteering for service since the breakthrough of unconditional love in my life. Now, because my friends in D.A. love me, I want to help them. I had helped my parents from time to time growing up, sure, but I didn't want to. And I threw fits about it and stole money from them because of it. But D.A. is teaching me to be honest and accountable for myself.

Recovery is about learning balance. When I work hard, I often feel pain afterward. I've often wondered why. The pain is a symbol that I am growing and healing. It is painful to move out of my comfort zone and take a risk. Where am I today? For one year I've written down my expenses, had a wonderful Pressure Relief Group, lived on my own, and had a sponsor to help me work the Steps. I am the first person in my family in many generations to make a home outside my home state. I am the first person in my family to live in an apartment of my own. I am proud of my home. It is the first of many visions to come true in my life. I have been employed full time, and my earnings are supporting me 100%. Slowly, with the help of my D.A. sponsor and Pressure Relief Group, I am learning that my parents don't owe me anything just because I feel they didn't do a good job. And these last months of supporting myself taught me that it feels much better when the money is my own. I can save with pride. I can make my own mistakes. After keeping track of my expenditures, I have two savings accounts with prudent reserves for three months' rent and living expenses. Three people in the last two days have asked me to sponsor them. And I once thought I had nothing to share. Thank God for D.A.

What Does a Family Have to Do With It?

A mother's desire to give her children "the best education
that money could buy" led to panic, then to D.A.

I tried the Debtors Anonymous program three times within three years, but I didn't continue. It didn't make sense to me. A friend from another program suggested I try D.A. after hearing me share at a meeting we both attended. I didn't think I belonged in D.A. Each time I went, I couldn't hear what was being said because of my state of panic. If I am in enough panic, I don't breathe right, and then I cannot hear. I already felt miserable over my bounced checks and debt to a private school. I knew I couldn't do anything to change my present circumstances, because I had tried.

How could I take our daughters out of that wonderful school where they were getting the "best education money could buy?" What would happen to us if we made a change? It was too unbearable to even think about, let alone take action to alleviate the financial strain it was causing me, my husband, and our children. When we ran out of money to finance the education, we began using our investments. First, our stocks and bonds, then our home equity. I was out of control. This school became the most important thing in my life. I believed I couldn't live with myself if I took our children out of it.

I couldn't find any full-time work. It was obvious I would need to go back to school. In the past, I had been a nurse, but it took too much energy to continue. I continued to bounce checks because I couldn't even balance a checkbook. I had to write such large checks for a habit I could no longer afford. Panic would set in, again!

It was November, which for me was a horrible time of the year. I always felt crippled from the rush and panic of the "shopping frenzy." I felt shame for not being able to buy my family the gifts all the other parents at the private school could afford to buy. I was angry and jealous. I prayed, but it didn't seem to help my anger and feelings of inferiority. I felt miserable and began using food to numb myself. Now I didn't know what to do. At the other Twelve Step meeting I attended, I ran into my friend, who again suggested Debtors Anonymous.

I "crawled" into D.A. and tried to listen. They were reading Step One and laughing hilariously. What was there to laugh about anyway? Weren't they in as much pain as I was? While listening to people share on this Step, I began daydreaming about my childhood. I seemed to remember my parents were "breaking, taming, and squelching" my spirit. They thought it was a healthy way to discipline. I was terrified at the thought of a broken spirit. How could anyone live without their spirit? I began to feel sick with shame. I felt as if everyone in that meeting was better than I was, and that I must stick out like a sore thumb. I thought about the shame I had felt about my two grandfathers drinking. I thought about my big family secret, incest. I was almost ready to pass out from panic when it was break time and someone came up and said, "Hello!" It was my friend from the other program. I stood up, she hugged me, and I started crying. Other people gathered around but didn't say anything. I was relieved. The pressure lessened as we spoke to one another. Then the meeting started again. After the meeting, I felt much better, in fact, remarkably better. I decided to "keep coming back."

I genuinely wanted to come back. I got a Pressure Relief Group and began working the Steps with a sponsor. Life became just like a miracle. I began attending more than one meeting in D.A. I volunteered for service. I found myself willing to take the treasury for the meeting I first attended. Now I didn't feel as much panic. We still sent our children to that private school, but I stopped bouncing checks. I could breathe, and I felt better.

Our General Service Representative announced at a meeting that she was attending the D.A. World Service Conference in Boston, and she needed funds to represent our meeting. She was on a special committee and wanted to do service at the world level. I volunteered to do service and organize a "Performance Night." This was a lot of work, but so much fun. When it was over, I could see how well we had done for our GSR, so I started to feel as if I could do service at this level too! I attended another D.A. meeting regularly, and they were willing to let me represent them. This was two weeks before the conference. At the monthly meeting, our GSR announced how well the fund-raiser went and that she could now go to Boston. I realized I wanted to go too. I was frightened, but raised my hand and said that I would love to go to Boston. All the other GSRs said, "You can! Just ask your group if they want to send you, and if they do, you'll go."

I left that meeting on a high and asked my own and other meetings to support me, and they did. I cried nearly every day as I opened my mail to find checks from people to send me to Boston.

While on the plane to Boston, I pinched myself to see if this was all real. I wanted desperately to do service, because I had been relieved of my panic. I felt I was in a dream world to be getting what I had asked for from the fellowship. I took my GSR position seriously. I loved doing service for D.A.

When I returned, I had new friends and a wonderful sense of myself. I had stopped using food to numb myself, along with staying out of debt. Now I felt I had everything to live for. My family and I moved to a different town; the children went to a public school. This miracle had happened to me. I saw that God was doing for me what I could not do for myself. The promise of recovery had come true for me and for my family.

Where did this disease begin and end for me? I don't know the answer, but I do know that having the willingness to "Keep Coming Back" helped me go from a state of panic to a state of grace. The blessings have been many. My growth sometimes feels like a rocket ship blasting off, and at other times like it is going at a snail's pace. This is the hardest program ever, yet I have grown the most in D.A. Through the help of others in D.A., Pressure Relief Groups, working with a sponsor, doing service, working the Twelve Steps, attending meetings, and most of all, prayer and meditation, I have been able to continue the road of recovery, one day at a time. I am a grateful member of Debtors Anonymous, and I pray to remain here until my last day on this planet. Thank you, D.A. and the living fellowship.

Recovery in New Hampshire

*D.A. was forty miles away, but it helped so much
that this debtor brought it home.*

Debtors Anonymous is the most gut-wrenching program I've ever encountered. At the same time, it offers hope and recovery from compulsive debting. It has forced me to examine hopes, dreams, fears and old beliefs, many of them well-hidden under a feast/famine mentality that I didn't even know I had.

When I came into D.A. eleven months ago, I was in pain and hopeless, buried under about $101,500 of secured and unsecured debt. At the outset, the vicious cycle of borrowing and repayment had seemed perfectly logical. Cash flow for my business had declined, and I had thousands of dollars of credit in bank credit lines and credit cards of every description and color, including gold, silver and platinum. I knew I was trustworthy and solvent, or these people wouldn't have advanced me this much credit. And that started the downward slide into ever-deepening debt, depression and fear; the worse it became, the more I debted until at the end I was practically immobilized.

For quite a while I hid, ostrich-like. The higher and higher levels of debt weren't due to department store spending or indulging myself in extravagances. In fact, when I hit bottom, only one department store card was affected. The debts were due to the attempt to keep my business afloat, marred considerably by an ego-driven business decision that cost plenty in money and forced me to really examine my egocentricity. Why else would one engage in a problematic business venture with a glib little-known business partner and no business plan? Since my mounting debt wasn't for "goodies" for myself, I rationalized that it really didn't count. There would always be more one more credit card to borrow from, cash flow would improve, the "big fix" would happen, and miraculously I would be saved.

This eventually came to a screeching halt. I was facing thousands of dollars of payments due or past due, with a cash flow at subsistence level, and creditors beginning to hound my every waking hour. It was then I found D.A. And it was then I made the inner commitment not to debt, no matter what, one day at a time.

The journey into recovery has been slow and decidedly erratic. I wish I could state that by following my decision, cash flow improved. That I made steady progress in paying off indebtedness, and that I've built significant cash reserves. None of that is true.

What did happen is that I cancelled credit cards and contacted all my creditors (a painful process), but I was getting threatening, harassing and intimidating phone calls from almost all of them. My cash flow remained very low. Even putting my own needs first—bare bones needs like paying rent and food—has been a daily struggle. Frequently, I had to juggle a car payment with money for the phone bill, robbing Peter to pay Paul.

That is the down side, but I have had many positives. My primary benefit so far has been that no matter what happened, I didn't debt one day at a time. Sometimes it was agonizingly painful, but I did learn. I learned how to participate in my own recovery. I work the program constantly. I keep spending records, spending plans and creditor contact logs. By recording my contacts with creditors, I discovered they often misrepresented what I had told them, or told me I had promised something I hadn't. Eventually I stopped phone contacts altogether and now insist on having all communication in writing. The more I took these steps, the more I realized my own power. It became clear to me that by my commitment to repay every cent I owe, I wasn't the "bad" or "deadbeat" person these collection people were addressing. This changed the tenor of our conversations. I learned, too, that their threats were just that, threats. If they had the power and authority they claimed, they wouldn't resort to intimidation. I learned to respond calmly in the race of their anger.

As frequently as possible I attend D.A. meetings. This isn't easy, because I live and work in a place where the closest meetings were about 40 miles away. Attending meetings might have cost me in time and gas, but making the effort was participating in my own recovery.

What became clear was that I needed support in my own area, and that led to a significant step in my recovery: starting meetings in my own area. I attended Intergroup meetings to learn how, and then started a D.A. group in my home town. Working independently, another person started a group in a town about 20 minutes away. We now work together supporting each other's meetings, giving Pressure Relief Groups, and trying to build D.A. in the state. I did the best

I could. I found a meeting place, put signs in shops around town, put a notice in our community newspaper, and showed up week after week, no matter what. Currently attendance at our meetings is growing, so the word about D.A. is getting out.

Finally, I began working on some of my more gut-wrenching issues. I realized that I had spent most of my life in the feast/famine cycle, going from no debt to increasingly huge debt, paying it off and starting over. There is still an active part of me that wants to continue this, but my commitment to the program is such that I no longer have to do this. Sometimes it is a struggle because the destructive part of me and my compulsive behaviors are still very much alive.

I looked at my spending and realized that the cause—whether I was borrowing to float my business or charging clothiers to dress nicely—didn't matter. My spending and debting were way out of proportion to reality. As one of my gifts of D.A., I came to realize that I could begin to balance income with outgo. Much of my spending had been "fix it," with "it" being anything from a disturbing encounter that day to my entire life. I used spending and debting to feel better, to appear grown-up and in control, and to make myself okay. All of these are addressed in D.A. Now I don't have to do those things. I can step back, think, and walk through uncomfortable feelings without debting.

With almost a year in D.A., even with a greatly reduced cash flow, I have reduced my debt to about $88,500. While that's a significant reduction, I still have a long way to go. But what I didn't understand when I first came into D.A. is that money is not the issue. What matters is the strength and recovery I have. I've learned that owing money doesn't make me a bad person. I've learned that in a business transaction they want their money, and I want to pay them. All we are discussing is how.

D.A. has given me back some control over my life and my finances. I've learned to stay positive, not to give in to the doubt and despair that comes with this compulsive disease. I've learned I do have a compulsive disease, but with the help of D.A. and my Higher Power, I can be healed. Thank you, D.A. Thank you, God.

The Wounded Bird

*At first credit cards were her safety net; they became a blinding web.
As she cut her way out, she found pain and reality.*

Debtors Anonymous is my main program. I read about it in 1989 in a magazine while I was on the way to Paris. I had a job there for four months with lavish benefits and excellent wages. The woman in the article said that in D.A. she learned to be financially responsible and how to stop the cycle of debting, that her life was prosperous now. I said, "I'll take some of that."

I determined to write down my numbers while I was in Paris. I kept track of my money the whole time. I was able to take some nice vacations while I was there, pay off an emotionally charged $5,000 loan, and shop sanely for presents for myself and others at the end of my stay.

Unfortunately, as soon as I returned to the United States, I completely forgot about Debtors Anonymous. I had $15,000 or more dollars in the bank. I could have written a check for half of my $30,000-plus debt and been left with only the student loans. Instead, I decided to start my own business. Happily, I rented an office and set out to find clients. Coincidentally, I stopped balancing my checkbook, not wanting to know when the money would run out. Thus, I began my cycle of debting in a more grandiose way.

I began to get credit cards with large lines of credit: $5,000, $7,500, and $10,000. I felt I deserved them; they made me feel important. I used one to make a down payment on a piece of property. Others I used to "finance" my business—there were employees to pay and clients that didn't pay at all. My debt grew past $60,000. I began to realize I was getting into hot water. I bought a taped version of a book recommending Debtors Anonymous and found my way to D.A.

I hated my first meeting. It was in the basement of a bank building in Beverly Hills. My subconscious criticized the gall of debtors who thought they were allowed to be in Beverly Hills. Further, the room was brown, there were no accountants or financial planners, and they talked about God. Yuck! It was not until the speaker told us about how he walked into a bank one day and signed for an unsecured loan for $1,000,000 that I knew I belonged. It also made my problems seem less life-threatening and led me to believe there might be life after debt. The speaker seemed like he had found it, so I thought that maybe I could too.

I went to meetings regularly, sometimes two or three a week. I cried a lot; I learned a lot. But I was still debting through Christmas and into the New Year. I had started writing down my numbers again, but hadn't changed any patterns. Then one day, after listening again to the tape on debt recovery, I realized I had to take the plunge and cut up my credit cards. A friend suggested I think of life without credit cards as "just an experiment"—something to try out. I could always go back. I had a lot of fear, and this felt like a bold and unsafe move. Who would take care of me if I didn't have my credit cards to rely on? Where would next month's rent come from? How would I pay my bills and student loans?

Within twenty-four hours of cutting up my credit cards, I started having memories of my brother and some neighborhood boys raping me. I was five. This had happened several times. I had not forgotten, but I had chosen never to think about it. Here these memories were, spooling through my brain like some lost film that threaded itself through my mental projector, so intent were they on being seen.

What was this all about? What an inopportune moment for such things to demand attention, just when I needed to button down and figure out how I was going to make ends meet! It started to drive me crazy. My bank account was dwindling, and the memories got more intense. The film expanded to include other kinds of abuse I suffered at the hands of family and neighbors—sexual, physical, emotional. By the time my bank account got down to $21, I couldn't stand the suspense and the craziness, and I took a cash advance for $2,000. The memories went away, and I had some peace, at least for a time—enough time to find help. I began therapy and to map out the path of my disease development.

My father is a debtor. As I was growing up, he would promise me shopping sprees with his credit cards once I turned sixteen. He never had his money figured out and frequently borrowed my savings on weekends, when banks were closed. His credit card bills were often past due. When I went to college, I got financial aid that included student loans. My father was thrilled. He said it was like "free money." As I signed on the dotted line, he said, "Don't worry, I'll help you pay it off if you have trouble." When I got credit cards of my own, he rooted me on, telling me my credit-acquiring skills far surpassed my brother's, who couldn't pay his bills on time or get a credit card. He said, "Since you have credit cards, I know you can take care of yourself." I knew I had attained that golden state of adulthood; I was considered "responsible."

My mother is also a debtor but in a pauperistic, compulsive-spending way. She is emotionally unstable and was one of my abuse perpetrators. The money lessons she taught me were: 1. The money just comes in and goes out; it never stays. 2. Our family was in the top 3% income in the nation, but we were poor. It is a mystery how this could be true. 3. I'm not allowed to have what I really want, but Mom will buy me five clearance items instead, though they are barely tolerable. 4. Food bills from the grocery store, country club, restaurants and school are always too high; I don't deserve to eat so much, and I should cut back. 5. Children shouldn't have extra spending money. This created a situation for my father to secretly give us spending money, but we couldn't tell Mom. This appeared to mean we didn't really deserve it, but he was making an exception. We should be appreciative of his sacrifice and good will.

When I was seventeen, my parents divorced, crumbling whatever foundation I had. I went off to college feeling alone and abandoned, with no home to go back to. As I developed a credit rating, credit cards became my safety net and provider. They helped me get through graduate school, travel around the world, and buy books, supplies, and clothes I couldn't afford. I felt important. I was a super-responsible debtor, always paying my bills before any other consideration. Toward the end of my debting, I incurred new debts to pay old ones. I tried to live within my means, but a workable budget seemed unfathomable to me, necessary only for those "boring" people who never went anywhere or did anything. For my lifestyle, credit cards were just tools I used to help myself along as I sank deeper and deeper into unreality.

Giving up credit cards and dealing with reality was really a shock. Not paying my debts if I had no money to pay them was a novel concept, but one my Pressure Relief Group insisted I try. It was excruciatingly painful to admit to my Ivy League university that I couldn't pay my student loans. I became an expert at moratorium letters and learned to deal with creditors. My credit report had gone from "responsible" to "bad risk," as I learned to become truly responsible to myself and my needs for food, shelter and self-care.

The greatest gift that D.A. has given me is the Twelve Steps. I went to an all-day workshop where we went through all Twelve Steps in one day. My incest issues were still fresh. By going through all the Steps in that one day, I could see how I had been harmed and how I had developed as a result of my wounds. It was most instructive to see how I had harmed others, my unpleasant personality traits, and to make a list of people I needed to make amends to. The notion that I, the victim, the wounded bird, owed apologies and needed to change my behavior blew me away. It was a shift of perception, my first real understanding of the concept of compassion.

Today, I don't debt, one day at a time. Over the last three years I have found that I debted in ways I had never imagined. I have learned what debting means. Debting used to make me feel worthwhile, since my abusive childhood had taken that away. I have been through a lot of therapy, gone to many meetings, and found support from other debtors working the program. I am learning to live again. I am so much more stable and strong that it is hard to remember how I could have been on my previous path.

Since joining Debtors Anonymous I have learned that life is more mysterious than I imagined. I know that I am enough; I am learning to feel it in every situation. Now I can see other people's compulsive patterns compassionately. I now see my own compulsive patterns. Sometimes I can stop them. I become aware of my fears, sit with them, get to know them. I am aware when other people are abusive, and I do not tolerate it. I refuse to be yelled at or beat up emotionally. I know when I am being abusive. Now I can change my patterns and stop harming others in order to satiate my wounded soul. I establish boundaries and communicate them. My job on the highway is to not hit anyone and to wish everyone a pleasant day. Beyond that, I can happily do anything that is legal. I no longer carry anger with me on my journey. I have found my spiritual path and gained a social conscience. Now I am honest, even when I think it isn't important. I have a new perspective on money, what it can and cannot do.

Progress, not perfection. I am cared for, and my old fears are leaving. God is my source. Today I am working on feeling my true value, all the way through to the deepest part of my soul. I thank God, for I am truly blessed. For this and for Debtors Anonymous, thank you, God.

Debt Was Hazardous to My Health

A major store gave this member her first credit card when she had no job, home or car. Soon she got others and used them until she couldn't imagine life without them.

Today I am wealthy and live prosperously. In just five years I have come from constant fear and contemplating bankruptcy to experiencing a sense of well-being and joy. It took a leap of faith to let go of my crushing dependency on credit and to trust that my security was dependent upon a Power greater than myself.

For me, it all started more than 25 years ago when I returned to my home state after my first two years in New York City. Until then, I worked only for myself, never considering using credit. When I got a job with a corporation, I borrowed $800 from the corporate credit union to buy a Chevrolet Custom Impala. The credit union painlessly withdrew monthly payments from my paycheck. When I sold the car a year later for $1,000, I paid off my loan in full. Little did I realize what long-term consequences a loan I could pay off would have. Little did I appreciate the freedom of a debt-free life.

The two categories of debt in D.A. are secured debt and unsecured debt. Secured debt has collateral, such as a house or car. D.A. addresses unsecured debt; that is, debt with nothing to back it up—debt with no collateral, such as credit card and personal loan debt. The car loan was the only secured debt I would have for the next 15 years.

In the midst of the summer I turned 26, I returned to New York with plans to start another business. I moved in with friends until I could earn some money for my own apartment. On a hot summer day, I detoured through a big department store to enjoy the air conditioning. A woman standing in the middle of a broad ground floor aisle stopped me and asked if I had the store's credit card. "Of course not," I replied. "Would you like one?" she asked. "Sure, why not," I said lightly. The air conditioning felt good, and I wanted to see the expression on her face when I told her my financial status. I was more than willing to give truthful answers to her personal questions: No job. No one supporting me. No house. No car. No apartment lease. No prior credit cards or bank loans. No private income. No assets. Nothing. Wait a minute, does a car loan from a corporate credit union count?

The address I gave her was in care of my friends, the clincher, I believed, to never getting that card. I didn't even want it. I didn't hope to get the plastic. I thought it was a big joke, and I was certain that I would not get the card.

The joke was on me.

That September I accepted a full-time job and soon used my grown-up, permanent job status and my department store credit reference to get lots more credit cards. Later I used my salary increases to take out debt consolidation loans from time to time to clean up my credit act. Although I had sincere-yet-brief intentions of never borrowing on those cards again, the debt consolidation loans only freed up my cards and other lines of credit for yet another spree of debting.

I was not criminally motivated, and I borrowed and charged with every intention of repaying my creditors. I knew that I earned as much as the next person, and that on my credit applications, I honestly stated my income, expenses, other lines of credit, and whether or not I owned a house or car. I figured the people who gave me credit knew something I didn't; for example, how I would get the money in the future to pay for the things that I just couldn't live without—not so uncommon in these days of instant gratification.

However, as my debt escalated, my monthly payments to my creditors used up more and more of my cash. Within a few years, the only way I could buy clothes, go out to dinner, or pay for entertainment was to use my credit card. Four years after I first applied for a credit card, I was using my credit cards to buy even groceries. At the time I earned about $15,000.

When I could admit and talk about my problem, a friend told me about a consumer credit counseling service. The next day I spoke with a counselor who took my $8,000 in bills, called my creditors, and negotiated a repayment plan with them all. I had only to send the service one monthly check, and they would send payments to my creditors. It was an almost painless way to solve the problem. Within a few years my debts were repaid, credit cards were mine to use again, and I was rewarded with bigger and better lines of credit. I had proven myself worthy of incurring a debt that was ridiculous in terms of my income, and then proven capable of repaying it. I had truly arrived as a good credit risk. I believed that as a seasoned credit card user, I had learned my lesson.

For six years, marriage intervened in my overspending habits. I set up our budget, because I was as acutely aware of my husband's extravagant spending pattern as I was blind to my own. Our money was shared. We both traveled extensively for work and had company expense accounts, relieving us of many of our day-to-day expenses. When we parted ways, he paid all our outstanding credit card bills. Once again I was left with a fist full of zero-balance credit cards.

For the next five years, I proceeded to incur over $25,000 of debt, including $2,200 in taxes. Fifteen years after I signed up for my department store credit card, I was working only three days a week and earned $36,000 annually, had an apartment lease, credit cards charged to the hilt, and two personal bank loans. I still had no house, no car, no one supporting me, no private income, no assets. I had begun a Master's program by borrowing money from my father, but could not continue my education with loans. My personal credit limit was used up, and I earned too much to qualify for school loans. My problem, I thought, was that my father would not pay for my education. It did not occur to me that debting was making my life unmanageable.

My debt load went from 53% of my annual income to 70% of my annual income in about ten years. I was in complete denial about my problem with debt. Often it became necessary for me to borrow from one card to pay another or periodically refinance my personal loan, called "debt consolidation." I paid the minimum balance every month, my rent, and heard no warnings about where I was headed, except from my accountant. Appalled at the interest I was paying for years, my accountant had advised me to pay off my credit cards. I justified the interest I was paying, because I wrote it off on my income taxes. He mentioned that soon interest wouldn't be deductible, if I needed further motivation to get rid of these lines of credit. He would roll his eyes, and I would ask myself, "What would you expect from a penny-pinching accountant? No nickel and diming for me, thank you very much."

The first time I sensed that I might have a problem with debt was when I applied for yet another debt consolidation loan and was refused. Even though I paid my monthly bills like the good citizen I knew I was, there was no cash left even to buy tokens to get to work and back. Whatever formula "they" used to figure my capacity to borrow against those credit limits, I was no longer able to repay even the monthly minimum. Something didn't compute. When I calculated what my basic monthly expenses were, including my monthly minimums,

I was shocked to realize that I could no longer live merely on a cash basis without being subsidized by a credit card. What was I thinking of? The answer is that I was not thinking, but that I was caught in the debtor's common symptom of "terminal vagueness." That glimmer of truth, however, did not change my debting habits.

My second awakening was sharp and powerful. Still oblivious to financial matters, I decided one day that I should start my own business. Not paying attention to financial details, I told my employer I would be leaving. That evening, I pored over my finances and became curious about how I might survive financially. That night I had nightmares about dinosaurs, land shifts, and impending doom. The next morning at the laundromat, I spoke to a friend about my financial concerns. He told me to stop paying my creditors, take care of myself, and start living on a cash basis. The creditors could wait.

He could have told me to walk to the edge of the earth and jump off, and I would have respected him more for his common sense. Where did this idiot live, anyway? Central Park? How could I abandon the creditors who had kept me afloat all these years, who had allowed me to vacation in Italy, who had sent me to retreats in California when I was feeling low, who fed, housed and clothed me for fifteen years? This guy was definitely a loser and didn't know what real life required.

However, I managed to listen when he told me about Debtors Anonymous, which I attended that very afternoon. The awareness that began to dawn the night before, as I combed over some rough figures, became ever so obvious when the veil was ripped from my eyes at that first D.A. meeting. I had a problem that was well-hidden beneath my monthly minimum payments. The real test was this: Could I live on a cash basis *and* pay my monthly minimums? The answer was no. This meant I would have to tell my creditors/safety net/substitute mommy-daddy/security blankets that their usual payments would not be forthcoming as we had agreed. I heard in D.A. that my creditors would not be happy with my decision, but there were ways that I could negotiate new payment terms and eventually pay back all the creditors on my terms. "On my terms" was an interesting new concept that would take on greater meaning as I progressed through the halls of Debtors Anonymous.

I cut up all my credit cards. It was very uncomfortable, and I felt deprived and vulnerable. My credit card lines and bank loans slid into default. I was on my own to start my own business and felt terror not knowing where the next paycheck would come from. Even after having the support of D.A. for five months, I went to a credit counseling service. I had hoped to turn my bills over to the credit counseling service so they could negotiate repayment with my creditors, as another service had done before. This time, however, because of my inconsistent and unpredictable income and disproportionate debt, I could not qualify for their debt repayment plan. Instead, they gave me information on bankruptcy.

With any addiction, we truly believe we cannot leave home or live without it. The "don't leave home without it" advertisements did not prepare me for what would happen when I had charged too much. I had never left home without "it." As a matter of fact, I never left home without "them." I also had a credit line attached to my checking account, which had the same effect as hamburger helper: It added bulk without substance. This all made me feel very secure that I would be able to cope with any emergency like take my nephews and nieces on a boat trip before it was "too late." I never asked myself, "Too late for what?"

I heard in D.A. that debting was like an addiction. After several meetings, I came to describe addiction as a negative state; for example, if I were addicted to alcohol, drugs or cigarettes, the absence of the substance would be felt as a deficiency. Without the substance, discomfort sets in until we regain our comfort level by using the substance. The discomfort comes from not using the addictive substance, and unwillingness to let go of it allows us to experience the tenacity of the addiction. I truly believed that neither I, nor anyone else, could live affluently without one or more credit cards or bank loans.

A warning on monthly bills might read: "If for some reason you are unable to comply with these terms and are unable to meet your monthly minimum or repay in full what you borrow, we reserve the right to turn your bill over to a collection agency that will emotionally and psychologically abuse you."

The collection agency is like a loan shark who would beat you up in the alley and threaten to murder you or your children if you don't repay the loan. The collection agency is restrained by law, but this doesn't stop them from working you over verbally on the phone, assaulting your character and attitude.

The collection agency threatened me with lawsuits and their counterpart to murder—*a bad credit rating*—without which, as we all know, we cannot live on this planet. They even said they were not lawyers and had no facts about what might happen. They just wanted to talk with me about why this happened. They talked to me as if I were a child, not letting me speak. They didn't speak about facts, only about me as a person—me as a bad person. One told me that people collecting welfare paid them more monthly than I was offering to pay. I was neither on welfare, collecting unemployment, nor employed, but it made no impression on them. They asked why I didn't have a job, what had I been doing about it. They insinuated that there was something definitely wrong with me, and they wanted to know what it was. Shame and hopelessness set in. They called a lot, never allowing much peace between their verbal batterings. The collection agency switched me from one representative to another, so no history, rapport or empathy could develop. They were just doing their job.

There is no debtor's prison, but after a few of these relentless, harassing phone calls, I wished there were. Maybe then I could escape the verbal and psychological abuse. I didn't discuss the problem with friends, because their disdain would be too demoralizing. The fear, shame and pressure from others, and especially myself, was paralyzing.

It was a nightmarish descent into debtor's hell. I already knew I was a social misfit because I no longer had a credit card, but now I had to experience degrading humiliation because I couldn't pay my monthly minimum. So what could I do? Commit suicide? Declare bankruptcy? Leave town and change my name, leaving no forwarding phone number?

In D.A. I heard debtors contemplate suicide as their first solution to debt. When I was younger and saw old newsreels of people jumping to their death because of the 1929 stock market crash, I couldn't believe it. "Just for money?" I wondered. Now I understand it.

The next solution commonly considered is bankruptcy. For me, it was a way to relieve the harassment exerted by collection agencies. Their taunts echoed my personal guilt and the cultural disdain for such failure. Armed with the Chapter 7 escape hatch, I went to D.A. and asked other members to give me a good reason why I should not declare bankruptcy. People in D.A. told me many good reasons. Much like my previous easy way out with the consumer credit service or my first husband taking care of "loose ends," anyone who is bailed out or goes bankrupt does not learn the lessons: How to live prosperously and happily on what you earn. How to acquire peace of mind. How to live independently of credit, which we have allowed to become the master of our lives. How not to be a victim. How to negotiate your own terms and resolve your own problems.

I had only unsecured debt, and therefore nothing to sell and nothing to lose. I did not pay any creditors for six months, relying on all the tools of D.A. to prevent me from caving in and going bankrupt. The tools are the Twelve Steps and the Twelve Traditions, along with practical suggestions. I went to lots of meetings, kept penny by penny accounts of my spending, learned how to create spreadsheets and spending plans, and began to learn how I could feel comfortable though earning much less than I had in the past. More than anything, keeping spreadsheets on my spending and creating a monthly spending plan made me see how I had always lived in fear of lack. I saw that even if I had earned more, I would still have been fearful about not having enough. I still would have made choices that reflected my fears. D.A.'s tools taught me how to make choices and feel more in control.

The biggest lesson I learned was that by relying on a Power greater than myself, I could let go of the fear. It was the fear that hurt me the most. I was often sick during that first year of D.A.; my stomach was in knots most of the time. For ten months in a row, on the first of the month, I had zero dollars in my checking account. But for ten months in a row, I was able to pay my rent, phone and electric bills, buy groceries, see a movie, and visit friends. The difference between my first month and the tenth month is that in the beginning I had been riddled with fear, could not sleep, was obsessed about money, and could not see a way out. After ten months, one day I looked at my zero balance checkbook, shrugged my shoulders and had a nice day. That night at a meeting I realized my fear had lifted. Money no longer could control how I felt or dictate to me if I was going to appreciate the positive things in my life. Removing fear of financial insecurity from my life is the greatest gift to me from D.A.

Eventually, with help from my D.A. friends, I began paying my creditors, sometimes only $10 or $15 a month...whatever was left after I took care of myself. Eventually, my creditors realized I would probably pay them back and the harassing phone calls and threats subsided. As my business grew and my income became more steady and reliable, I increased my monthly payments to creditors.

It's been five years now since I entered D.A. and stopped using credit cards. Today I owe $8,000 compared to the original $25,259 of debt. My father forgave his loan to me. I negotiated a two-year payment plan to pay back my overdue taxes. I consolidated and refinanced my personal bank loans for a better interest rate and more manageable monthly payments. All of my retail store debts are paid off. My business is booming, and my current plan is to retire all of my debt in sixteen months. I didn't have to hide behind an agency who would talk to my creditors for me. No matter how fearful I was of the collection agencies, I learned that they couldn't really hurt me. Even if they had sued me, which none did, a court hearing wouldn't have frightened me. I am now certain that not only can I repay all of my debt, but I will be able to save money instead of paying enormous amounts of interest. It's a miracle.

Since coming to D.A., I have paid my rent and utilities every month, eaten well, enjoyed vacations and entertainment, returned to graduate school to finish my Master's degree, and paid cash for everything including my computer and spreadsheet software. The spreadsheet allows me to keep a penny by penny account of my finances and reveals a great deal about the choices I make in my life. I also learned that a debit card, which looks and acts like a credit card but deducts the purchase amount directly from my personal checking account, takes care of car rentals, hotel reservations, and other purchases that require plastic.

The big difference is not in the lesser dollar amount I owe, but rather that since D.A., I have lived on a cash basis, after fifteen years of the illusion that credit cards were taking care of me. In fact, I had been taking care of the lending institutions by paying so much interest. The focus of D.A. is taking care of myself. D.A. taught me that if I didn't learn to take care of myself, then I could not take care of anyone else. Without D.A. I would not have been able to reverse the process of incurring debt or learn how to live a debt-free and prosperous life. My peace of mind became essential to the process, and I needed my supportive and understanding program friends. They too have felt the embarrassment and humiliation of being in the same place...in debt.

I as a debtor was not guilty, per se. I did, however, have to take responsibility for changing my self-destructive behavior. I needed help in a nonjudgmental, safe place. I have the benefit of D.A., for without it I never would have been able to let go of my credit cards overnight. Without D.A., I never would have trusted myself to survive without a line of credit. In D.A. I learned to manage my money, no matter how much or how little. Although I started out hoping I would be one of those in the fellowship who triples income or becomes rich, I realize that at whatever level I earn money, I can make choices about whether or not I will enjoy abundance in my life. No longer is there a false sense of security based on any person, place, circumstance, or line of credit. The saying, "The best things in life are free," is no longer an empty cliche´.

To believe that I could live without debting took a leap of faith from the common beliefs in this society, beliefs that are bolstered by a lot of advertising about things I should want or need and about the credit lines that will get them.

My freedom becomes greater every day, because I make choices about what I really need to live fully and what is important: my well-being, joy and peace.

Free of the Golden Cage

After starting to work the program alone, she joined with others to start meetings and with their support, found independence from her family's wealth.

"I come from a hurtful family."

I heard someone say that in a D.A. meeting, and I knew that I was home. I too come from a "hurtful family." And the weapon used most often is money. Money is used to control. It is used to abuse, and it is used as a bribe to keep you within the invisible limits. I look back at my childhood and now tell people it was like growing up in a golden birdcage…the cage was beautiful, and it looked like we had all that money could buy. We did. Yet we were trapped and controlled and brainwashed.

Today, I am the only bird who has discovered that the key was in the cage all the time. The key was belief. Belief that the world outside was warm and welcoming. Belief in a Higher Power that was not a menacing cat. Belief that wings never used can be strengthened by learning from other birds that have learned not only to fly, but to soar higher than they ever knew was possible. Belief that I am my source. Not my parents, husband, or employer.

Hanging on to this belief is my goal in D.A. I was told as a child and young adult, "It is a cold, cruel world out there. The only place you are safe is here."

My father is an adult child of an alcoholic. The world he knew was cruel. Poverty, violence, and abuse were his experience. I know today that he meant well by keeping me in the cage; he was only trying to keep me safe.

I have learned in D.A. that we create our own safety. It is not something someone else can do for us. But we can do it together. Here is some of my story. How it was, what happened, and what it is like today. I hope that reading it helps you create your own safety.

My first debt was for $400. I was 18 years old. Having had no career preparation, I was a prime candidate for what my co-sponsor and I now call "those multi-level marketing companies." One was particularly appealing. It promised cars, fur coats, diamond rings, and *attention*. What I wanted most of all was to be noticed. My dream was to be on stage...

I spent ten years trying to achieve what I could not believe. There was a saying, "You haven't failed until you've quit." I didn't quit. I didn't want to be a failure.

I did, however, lose everything I had, including my money, husband, baby, company stock, and sanity. I was committed to a mental institution (that's what they were called before they called them treatment centers) wearing a leather suit and $15,000 in debt.

I did get to go on stage. It was the most expensive two minutes of my life!

My brother bailed me out. My brother always had more than enough cash because of our family tradition of men getting all the money and women being expected to marry well.

Years before, I had been diagnosed with manic depression; I was taking lithium when this incident occurred. As you can see, lithium didn't work very well. My days in the hospital were a nightmare that still has not faded. I am grateful that episode landed me in the office of a neuropsychiatrist.

My proper diagnosis was "temporal lobe epilepsy." It is treated with seizure medication. With seizure medication I am as "normal" as I am ever going to get. There are few side effects, and I can now do things I consider miracles, even though they are commonplace for others.

The same doctor also diagnosed me with ADD, or attention deficit disorder. I also take medication for that, and the chronic mess and clutter that plague my existence on this earth have slowly begun to disappear. If I forget a dose, it reappears right in front of my very eyes!

All of this happened before I knew about D.A. I wish I had known about it when I was in debt. As it happens, I did not know, and my pain and shame were tough to bear. I tried sharing about these issues in my other Twelve Step program, but they looked at me as if I was in the wrong room. I was.

Three years ago, I read a book about D.A. I felt relief and a sense of lightness wash over my body. I felt like I was no longer alone on the planet. There were others like me. Some had done even crazier things. Some had larger debts ($240,000 sticks out in my mind). I was determined to find this Debtors Anonymous.

Well, I did. The problem was that the only meeting was in a nearby city at 6:00 p.m. So much for that. I don't drive in cities. And I had two small children eating dinner at 6:00 p.m. and a husband who was still at work.

I decided to start working the program alone.

For three months, I wrote my money down every day and did not debt, no matter what, one day at a time. My finances and our family's finances began to change. It was amazing.

I went to a conference and a meeting with two other D.A. members. It was wonderful! I wanted more. I found one member from my state, a room showed up, and we started a meeting with three people. We even dragged in a newcomer for our first meeting. About four months later, we had grown to 25 members. We sponsored each other and talked on the phone. We weren't rigid with rules. After all, we were all we had. We mostly loved each other and struggled together. We read the literature. We played tapes that had shown up somehow and used that as experience, strength, and hope.

To me the best thing we did was treat each other with gentleness. If one of us made a mistake, another would say to forgive and be gentle.

I inherited some money, and it stayed in the bank! I used the interest for a trip to a World Conference. I brought back whatever I could, especially enthusiasm.

It took about two years for me to realize that my hidden problem was under-earning. I had been so deprived as a child in some ways that keeping myself at zero was comfortable.

I started doing little things. Keeping the gas tank at F instead of E. Keeping money in my wallet and in my checking account. Asking for what I wanted. Ordering what I wanted on a menu, not just the cheapest thing. Keeping food in the house. Buying two, not just one.

Two years into D.A., I got bored. I was out of debt. I was almost done with the Master's degree that I had started seven years before. I felt stuck.

One of the things I had learned in sales was to make a "goal poster." I thought I would try it again. I took old magazines and cut out pictures of things I wanted. I pasted them on a big sheet of cardboard and colored affirmations. I put in some easy ones this time. In the past I had always had huge goals and would give up in a week if they did not happen. This time I put some manageable ones in like good grades and smiling children. I sprinkled it with glitter. I put a picture of thin thighs and vegetables. I added a symbol that represented my Higher Power and asked that only the ones that are for my highest good be manifest.

I hung up my poster and waited. I did the footwork, like going to class when sleeping in would have been have been easier. The goals started to come true. It is now two years later and most have come true, except the long-term ones.

I told a friend about my poster. The result was the beginning of a Visions meeting.

I realized I had been frustrated in D.A. I was married and did not have any income of my own. It is difficult to have a spending plan when you have nothing to spend. No wonder I was frustrated.

The changes in my life from Visions are incredible. A job appeared. It was only four hours a week, but it was in the field I wanted, so I took it. Soon it increased to 20 hours a week. I started getting sloppy with my regular program; the job went down to 17 hours a week. I started over again. The job became an offer of full-time work with great benefits. The money was terrible. I told the person I could not do it for that salary. I prayed and let it go. Eight hours later, $2,000 was added to the salary. I negotiated the hours and took the position. In the middle of this grueling process, I got a sponsor. There are no coincidences, just miracles in which God chooses to remain anonymous.

Today life is a joy, not a burden. I look forward with expectancy to the journey ahead. I know with certainty that it will be the path that my Higher Power has chosen for me as long as I choose to listen to my inner voice and make healthy choices. It awes me that I wrote this story. One of my visions is to be a writer. As with so many other things, I guess I already am. I just have to claim the gift as mine and use it for the highest good.

There are downsides, too. It is difficult to see the rest of my family have so much money. My brother is a millionaire, and I cannot seem to let go of my belief that he took so much from me. My parents are the true holders of responsibility, as it was their decisions that allowed our family wealth to be distributed as it is. I still get angry at God when I feel that I do not have enough. Christmas is a tough time of year. The presents are so out of balance.

When the fear rolls in, I replace it with faith. They have more money, yet I am wealthy. I am free. No one controls what I buy, how often I work, when I rest. I watch them work 18-24 hours a day at times, and I am grateful for the peace in my life. I love my job. I love being in a place where I am respected and valued. I don't have as many things as my family, yet the things I do have I cherish and maintain well. And I believe that for whatever reason, this is where I belong.

The greatest gift of all is being able to help my children. They have allowances, but it is not taken away if they do not behave. My nine-year-old has a spending plan and a savings account. My four-year-old gets an allowance and is learning not to spend it all on video games. They help around the house, because it is their home. When they are tired, I have them stop and rest. They are never punished with money. They are already thinking about college—and even graduate school! They see the craziness in our families and get to talk about what they feel. They know the difference between wants and needs. And through helping them grow, I am finally growing up myself. Thank you, D.A.

The Good Old Days: A Fond Look Back

D.A. was his last resort; it became his first investment.

One Sunday about seven years ago, I awoke from a long, dreamless sleep and found myself $20,117.96 in debt—to six credit cards, many friends, student loans, my bank, and to my nemesis, the Department of Motor Vehicles.

I didn't know how it all had happened. I was truly mystified. All I knew was that I was a trustworthy and decent human being, that I had not intentionally set out to make friends and total strangers upset, impatient, frustrated, and angry with me. I never seriously entertained the idea of running out on my debts or "beating" my creditors; I had every intention of repaying money I borrowed and spent. I believed that a combination of unfortunate circumstances—a bad childhood, a few bad relationships, an illness, car problems, a job loss, graduate school, a career change, a lousy job market, and an eventual low-paying job—had made it impossible for me to avoid going into debt. In sum, I was the most misunderstood and maligned person on earth.

On the other hand, I knew exactly how it had all happened. By the time I was out of college, I was already bouncing checks and borrowing against credit cards. I had never lived where I paid the rent on time. My mood-changing shopping sprees, my spending for status, my poor financial judgment, my equating love with money, my anxious wait for the Big Fix, my denial, my rationalizations—all these and more I knew to be true on a gut level, but they hadn't reached my soul yet.

I didn't know what to do. Terrified, I was literally penniless. I had incoming bills that I couldn't pay, a car that was out of gas and needed maintenance, and an empty refrigerator. Believe me, I tried to borrow more money. Though on some level I knew it was impossible to get out of debt by borrowing more money, all that concerned me then was basic survival. Borrowing was the only way I knew to get by. I begged my bank to lend me more money; I pleaded with my credit card companies to raise my credit limits (how humiliating!), but my efforts were in vain. No one would lend me another dime. My "debt-to-income ratio" was too high. And now as I look back, that was a blessing in disguise.

I had known of Debtors Anonymous for nearly a year before I joined. I first heard of it in a graduate course on addictions and substance abuse. "Hmmm, Debtors Anonymous," I mused somewhat sarcastically. "Sounds like something I could use." Purely out of curiosity I decided to attend a meeting, but as fate would have it, when I arrived I learned the meeting had been moved to another location. Deciding a late arrival would be too embarrassing, I opted to return the next week. As it happened, I returned the next year. Again, as I look back, I was not meant to go to that first meeting. I was still in the heyday of my debting and hadn't hit bottom yet. "D.A. is my last resort," I told myself. "If I really screw up, then I'll go." And did I screw up!

That following year, I attended my first D.A. meeting. I was extremely arrogant. In retrospect, I don't know how anyone put up with me. I thought that my expenses were extraordinary, that I wasn't some deadbeat who didn't pay my bills: Once I graduated and got a real job I'd really rake in the bucks. Hell, I'd show them! I didn't keep a spending record or have a spending plan, and I still used credit cards. Even outside of D.A., all I ever talked about were bills and money.

Gradually, however, things began to change. I was starting to internalize what I heard at meetings. This was not conscious—I was listening with my soul. Outside of D.A., in my other life I noticed subtle differences in my thinking. I wasn't so uptight and impatient, so bitter and resentful. Amazed, I eventually realized that I wasn't doing anything that I enjoyed. No wonder I was so depressed and lethargic! Either I was doing what I thought others expected of me, or I was living for others because of my inability to set boundaries, or I was debting to take my feelings away.

D.A. taught me these truths: Just because I don't have everything I want doesn't mean I have nothing, money can't buy what money can't buy, and it just couldn't buy what I was missing. Spending to fill that soul emptiness wasn't going to work. Instead, I filled my soul emptiness with actions and quickly discovered that the emptiness closed up. Now I enjoy what is mine, both my material possessions and my personal attributes. My life has become fulfilled.

My debts, the reason I came to D.A., are slowly coming under control. I have negotiated repayment agreements with my personal creditors, took forbearances on my student loans, and paid off every outstanding parking violation. I have a commitment not to incur any new ones. My personal bank loan was paid up last week. I glowed as I wrote the last check. I paid off five of my six credit cards; four of them had reached the limits. Now the cards are destroyed, and my accounts are closed. Instead of the fear and defeat I anticipated when I cut up the cards, I felt freedom and relief. I have liquidated over $4,000 of my debts at this point, all without any sense of deprivation. I even went on a much-needed two-week vacation and paid in cash. I keep a daily spending record and a monthly spending plan, tools I scoffed at when I first came to D.A. Strangely, I never realized how much I actually earned until recently.

All of these gifts are beyond my wildest dreams. When I was debting, my life consisted entirely of deprivation and pressure, but this trip down memory lane has been revealing and rewarding. Now I know how far I've come in ten months of D.A. recovery and how far I still have to go. This journey has not been easy. All of my character defects and compulsions revolve around money. Through D.A., I learned that money itself is not the problem. The real problem is the issues money brings up. Transforming my miserable existence in a meaningful life is nothing short of miraculous. Now I can look forward to the future instead of dreading it. I'll live better, not worse, than I did in the old days. And for these gifts I have D.A. to thank.

How I Learned To Love What I Have

"Shopping, spending and charging to hide my real and perceived deficiencies consumed my every waking moment."

D.A. has shown me the real nature of my compulsive debting, how and why I used it to hide my true nature and deny myself tranquility. In D.A. I learned that my debting had cruelly twisted my character, exaggerating my defects and distorting my strengths. Activities that were once a source of pleasure and self-esteem became travesties causing me more regrets than fond memories. Rediscovering that pleasure has returned fulfillment and prosperity to my life.

Avid reading has been a lifelong hobby, ever since age two, when I taught myself how to read. Now I average about 200 books per year. Before my full-blown compulsion to buy and spend manifested, I borrowed all the books I read from the public library, buying only those I sincerely loved. I remember how proud I was to get my very first library card, a child's card that let me borrow two books a week. How excited I was to attain the coveted status of *adult borrower* at age 12 when I could borrow ten books a week! And I read them all, cover to cover, even the ones I didn't particularly like. I would spend weekends in the library, gazing rapturously at the stacks, wondering if there was enough time in the universe to read them all. I remember being known personally to the librarians, first as the child who checked out beginning astronomy texts, then as an adult who checked out everything from Jacqueline Susanne to Fyodor Dostoyevsky.

Getting my first credit cards changed all that. Not my tastes, certainly, but my motivations. While I was debting, I bought hundreds of books on my credit cards instead of borrowing them from the library. My rationalization was: "I have to build up a respectable personal library or no one will believe I really know anything. Besides, there's never any parking at the library." Instead of knowledge for its own sake, knowledge was for impressing my friends, showing off how smart I was. Buying books even became a race to see who could buy the complete works of an author first. And not the paperbacks, mind you, those were "worthless." To be an authentic aficionado, you must possess the leather bound, gold leaf, autographed editions, or else you were merely a dilettante.

The result was *I ceased to read for myself.* I stopped an activity essential to my well-being. It was no longer a source of pleasure. It felt like a chore, and it really was, now that I think about it. Combing through newspapers and mail order catalogs for obscure titles, going to all the trouble of shopping and buying them, lugging them home in a backpack, and then finding space for and shelving them alphabetically by subject and author was downright exhausting. It's a miracle that I even read the comparative few that I did.

However, and this is the really sad part, once I got the books home, most of them would sit on a shelf untouched. Worse yet, I'd "forget" I'd bought them and would buy duplicates, triplicates even. In bookstores I would get this overpowering urge, although mere words don't describe it: "I just *have* to buy this! The world will come to an end if I don't!" Then I would charge it. It was lycanthropy, some raving bibliophilic werewolf. When I left the store, my heart would pound. I had all this great stuff, but as soon as I got home and shelved them, I never gave them a second thought.

Consequently I didn't *enjoy* my library or any other compulsive purchases. Shopping, spending and charging to hide my real or perceived deficiencies consumed every waking moment. From books, my compulsion spread to albums and cassettes, from music to videotapes, from cookbooks to eating out. I lost sight of my identity. I was too busy trying to disguise it, suppress it, and change it. I desperately needed to say, "Wait a minute! What am I doing? This is all wrong!" Only in D.A. could I say that, and I did.

Reading isn't the only thing I've rediscovered. Cooking for myself, instead of eating most of my meals out, is also something I enjoyed in the past. Instead of bragging that I've eaten in every restaurant in my city at least once, I can demonstrate my resurrected cooking skills. Why not? I have forty cookbooks. Writing in my journal and volunteering for social organizations are other ways I now occupy my time.

Quality superseded quantity. I began downsizing everything, sorting, discarding, donating to charity, and reorganizing. Years of compulsive spending accumulated mountains of stuff with hardly any effort at all. Attacking my closets, drawers (all were junk drawers), bookshelves, under-bed storage, basement storage, and car was exhausting, but exhilarating. My home sighed in relief.

Quality is not restricted to possessions, however. I try to spend my time as quality time, my communications as quality letters and phone calls. Amazing how many treasures lurk amid the trash.

As for what I don't have, I don't have it. It's that simple. It doesn't mean I'm worthless. It doesn't mean I'm stupid. It doesn't mean I have nothing. What a simple, yet profound realization! How long did it take me to realize this? "Too long," I joke. Yet each of us takes all the time we need. There are no shortcuts.

I still *love* to spend money. That's what my disease is, and I accept it. Fighting it did me no good. Whenever I go shopping for anything from toothpaste to a winter coat, my heart pounds and my spirits rise. Once in a store, even though I have a list, I still find myself wandering around looking at everything else that I don't need, searching for excuses to buy something else, anything. Sometimes I think of all the money I wasted on restaurants, cabs, books, and credit card interest, and I become angry and sad. Sometimes I feel overwhelmed by my outstanding debts.

Whenever I get these feelings, I no longer try to stuff them. I acknowledge their existence and check my D.A. list for a meeting. Finally, after long and fruitless searches, I have attained a tranquility that I believed to be a myth. Now I know my problem is not money itself but the issues that money brings up. My financial crises were but symptoms of some underlying disease. The intangibles of D.A., much to my astonishment, are more valuable than a bigger checkbook balance. A year ago someone tried to tell me that, and I think I laughed.

I'm sure we've all had something we loved and then lost to our compulsions. Take the time to find it. It still works. You'll see.

Dependent On Plastic

A compulsive shopper breaks out of a family pattern of secrecy.

I am a compulsive spender and debtor in recovery. Two years ago I had $15,000 of credit card debt. At that time my marriage was falling apart. My husband had always bailed me out before, but this time he said he was tired of being my "enabler" and he wouldn't come through for me again. He gave me six months to make radical changes in my life or our seven-year marriage was over. Fortunately for me and our two children, I took him seriously. I haven't used credit cards or incurred any new debt for more than two years, one day a time.

I grew up in the South in an upper middle class family. As long as I can remember, my parents argued about money. My mother would write checks and ring up her credit cards and expect my father to pick up the tab. It was obvious to my two older sisters and myself that our mother should discuss her purchases in advance with my father, rather than waiting for him to receive the bills and hit the roof. It was ironic that as an adult, I would find myself repeating the same pattern with my own husband.

Some of the messages about money that I learned as a child were:

1) If you feel sad or depressed, go shopping and buy some new clothes. You will immediately (if temporarily) feel better.

2) Don't worry if you can't afford to buy what you want immediately. Go ahead and buy it. There will always be someone to bail you out later.

3) Keep your debts a secret. Over the course of many years, my mother would secretly spend money she didn't really have. Then she'd try to hide the extent of the damage from my father.

The best, or worst, example of my mother's secrecy about money was when my older sister was getting married and planned what I call a "pageant" wedding. My father had become blind before his death and needed my mother to pay the bills and manage their money.

My father had agreed to a budget of $7,000 for my sister's wedding. Our whole family thought it was fair. Years later, we learned that my mother had actually spent closer to $30,000 without my father's knowledge, or anyone else's for that matter. In hindsight, I think my sister would have preferred the cash. There were a few clues that my mom was overspending, like her paying for all ten bridesmaids' dresses and shoes, an expense ordinarily covered by the bridesmaids. Having a "spending plan" for the wedding and comparing budgeted to actual expenditures would have been a foreign concept to our family.

Before I became a grateful member of Debtors Anonymous, I had grown up to be surprisingly like my mother. I would go shopping when I was sad or angry, rather than expressing my true feelings directly, and I would rush each day to get to the mailbox so I could hide the credit card bills from my husband.

I always loved to shop at the large expensive department stores, still do, because the sales people are so solicitous. Never mind that they are motivated by the commissions they are hoping to make; the important thing is I feel pampered and respected. For someone who suffers from low self-esteem, it can be nice to hear a stranger say, "Oh, that looks great on you!" I would pretend I was a really wealthy person, and these purchases were just a trifle to me. It was great if the salesperson played along with my game, deferring to me in that certain way reserved for the rich and famous. I used to feel so important when I would open my wallet and choose a credit card from among the many I kept there. Even if I was using a credit card, I wanted everyone to know I had a gold card and would receive my platinum card in the mail any day. When I saw those credit cards lined up in my wallet, I felt rich and successful. I didn't feel I was enough without the plastic to show as proof of my worth. Poor people pay with cash, but rich people always charge everything, right? Wrong.

I remember when my debt was getting larger, and I had reached my limit on several credit cards. I had to remember my balances on each card to make sure I didn't present one that would be declined. It was getting a little stressful to go shopping. Guilt and shame were overwhelming as I would wait to hear if my credit card had been accepted. Strangely enough, I usually knew if I was close to my limit on each credit card and what my credit limits were, but I was often vague about the total amount of my debt and unclear about whether or not I could afford a particular purchase. It seemed worth it all, however, when I would leave department stores with new clothes wrapped in tissue and placed in shopping bags.

Once I got home with my purchases, I would try to slip the clothes into my closet without my husband noticing. I would cut off all the price tags immediately. Then I would slowly introduce different pieces of clothing throughout the next several weeks, always pretending these clothes had been in my closet all along, that I just hadn't worn them in awhile. I would do the same with my friends when they would compliment me on a purchase—I would pretend that I had bought it a long time ago, that they just had not seen it before.

Aside from my compulsive shopping, I would draft large sums of money from my credit cards to pay monthly bills. My husband and I had arbitrarily decided that $2,500 seemed like a lot of money, enough to cover most monthly expenses. So, when I didn't have enough money in my account to pay the telephone bill, for example, I would assume it was my fault. I would draft money from a credit card to pay the bill without my husband's knowledge. Once we were able to sit down and create a budget or spending plan together, we realized it actually cost closer to $5,000 per month to pay the bills for our family of four. I had been debting unnecessarily.

The worst part about using credit cards for me was when the bills came. I would rush to the mailbox each day to beat my husband, keeping him in the dark. After a while, he just assumed that I always collected and sorted the mail each day because I liked to. Little did he know how painful it really was. The reality of my overspending was there in black and white, plus 18% interest. I was usually able to pay only the minimum balance due.

Jung has said that "healing comes in relationship," and that has certainly been my experience. The biggest benefit of D.A. for me is just coming together week after week to be myself with other people who are willing to share themselves openly and honestly with the group. It is so important for me to be reminded that I am not alone.

Many people in D.A. have also said over the years, "We are only as guilty as our secrets." I have found this to be true. Confessing the full extent of my financial difficulties first to my husband, then to my therapist, and then to the members of my D.A. meeting were crucial steps in my healing process. It was important for me to say the exact amount of my debt and to be specific about how the money had been spent.

Another important action for me was cutting up all my credit cards. Six months before I had "bottomed out," I cut up all my cards except one. I rationalized that since the bill had to be paid within thirty days, I couldn't get into serious debt. The reality was that I would overspend on my credit card and borrow from other sources to make payments. I have come to realize that if I don't have enough cash to buy something, then I can't afford it. Also, if I consider buying something that costs over $100, I need to discuss it first with my husband. Even if he agrees, however, I have learned it is important for me to wait 24 hours before making a major purchase. Then I can feel good about what I buy and not worry that I have bought something compulsively.

Letting go of that last card was symbolic for me. It meant I no longer needed to get my sense of self-worth from a piece of plastic. It meant I would live within my means each month and not have a crutch to fall back on. It meant I was ready to act like a "grown-up" and take responsibility for my financial life.

To commemorate my graduation from credit cards, I took the cut up pieces and made them into a collage. On the left side of my collage is a man surrounded by credit cards and drowning in a can of tomato soup. On the right side of the collage is a tribute to "honesty and willingness." Included are pictures of what my Higher Power has come to represent for me, such as a mountain for strength, a whale for depth. These qualities are not outside of me, but I now realize are hidden within.

I also have a picture of *Beauty and the Beast* in my collage. For years, I lived a life of quiet desperation. I have always been a people pleaser, learning at an early age to discern what others want and need, often without regard for my own needs or desires. It was important that I appear competent and perfect, because I felt so unworthy and inadequate. I am still afraid sometimes that if I show my true self, complete with imperfections, no one could really love or respect me. As I strived for perfection and presented a managed personality, a beast inside me would periodically flare up and express itself through my compulsive spending and debting. Not until I was willing to face that beast and admit to being only human was I able to get a sense of who I really am. I am just beginning to learn what I want and need for the first time in my life. By facing the beast, it can be transformed into something really interesting and beautiful.

When I first came to D.A., I wasn't sure I had anything in common with most of the people in the room. I wanted to get rid of my affliction, get out of debt, and move on as soon as possible. Now, I am completely out of debt and record my expenses every day. I understand now what people mean when they say D.A. is not really about the money. Getting my finances in order is only one piece of the program. In a way, solvency is a mere side effect of working the

Twelve Steps and realizing the spiritual implications of being a debtor. I now know I have something in common with every person who attends a D.A. meeting, regardless of their financial situation. The beast within me will always be there, but it is out of the shadows of denial and secrecy. The light of awareness has permanently altered the landscape of my life, and I will forever be grateful.

By the way, I still love shopping and the smell of new clothes, but now I feel fantastic when I buy something I can afford and pay cash. Keep coming back. It works!

Rebellious and Resistant

She went from welfare to six figures, debting all the way. In D.A. she learned that while the money had changed, she hadn't.

I'm not one of those people who waltzed into D.A. with hope shining in her eyes. I hated it, I didn't want to be there, and I was happy to tell you at length just how much I hated it.

I am primarily a pauper. I have a college degree, and training in various fields of communication, but I wasn't able to get an entry-level job in my field. I had refused to learn to type, so after graduation my jobs had included vacuuming floors for a large commercial cleaning firm, door-to-door canvassing for a political group, and being a sales clerk and cage cleaner in a small pet store. None of these positions paid more than minimum wage; some paid less.

When I got a job in advertising sales, I felt like I was moving up. The newspaper I worked for was small and barely paying the bills. I was trying to sell advertising on straight commission. Without a car, public transit ate up a lot of my time. I am not a good salesperson, so my commissions were neither high nor steady. My pay was based on my actual receipts, so I never knew whether my weekly paycheck would be $20 or $500. I was supposed to be paying my own taxes quarterly, but I never did. There was never enough to do that, if I was to eat and pay rent, too.

My student loans were badly in arrears, along with back phone and utility bills. When I moved into the house I shared with friends, none of the bills could be in my name, since no utility company would have me until I paid up and made a substantial deposit. I had many creditors whose mail I never even opened—it all went into a drawer. Any time I was home in the daytime, I screened my calls. I borrowed small sums from friends and family, paying them back off the top of the next paycheck, so each paycheck was already spent when I got it. If it was a $20 week, my paycheck was gone, and then some.

I didn't sleep nights. I was like a little kid cut loose with no instructions. I was terrified, bitter, resentful and confused. I felt that I had failed. I couldn't see how anything could change for the better, but I could easily envision worse.

I had almost a year in two other Twelve Step programs, and I attended five to seven meetings a week. I felt like I was already doing plenty, so I resisted D.A. like crazy. At the first meeting, I found things to complain about: They charged for the literature, they held their meeting in a psych ward, they didn't say, "We ask newcomers not to contribute for their first three meetings" like the other programs, they held long tedious business meetings. There's more—I just knew they were doing it all wrong.

So I went one week, stayed away the next, went back the next, kicking and screaming all the way. Every other week for months I showed up, cranky, resistant and sullen. The first few times, I just sat there. After that I started to share. My first few shares were full of rage, tears, and bitterness. It was all D.A.'s fault that I was in so much pain. If they were doing it right, like the other programs, I wouldn't be having such a hard time.

To my chagrin, the people in the meeting didn't take offense when I raged. Several of them even thanked me after the meeting for being honest. Their support didn't make the pain any less, but it did help me to keep coming back. Though I hated the meetings, I knew I needed to be there.

It took me a long time to figure out that my pain and the flaws in the meetings were separate issues. In fact, I stayed just long enough to "Twelve Step" my sponsor from another program into D.A. Then I left for several months. When I came back, the meeting had moved into a church basement. Now there were more people with Twelve Step backgrounds, gently turning the meeting toward the traditions. And that felt better.

But this had nothing to do with my rebellion and rage. If the meeting had been perfect, filled with Twelve Step angels, I would still have been in pain. I would have been angry, because everyone was too good. I still don't know why facing that I was powerless over money was so much more difficult and painful than my other problems—it just was. And still is, sometimes. My rebellion has not vanished—it's just quieter.

When I came back, I began to hear what people shared. I also began to share honestly without being so combative. I stayed for business meetings and contributed to the group. For a while, I opened and closed the meeting, chaired meetings, talked to newcomers, and I settled down just a little. I started keeping records, but for a long time I didn't tally them.

I found work I liked that wasn't commission, paying slightly better than the newspaper did. Now I could open all my mail. I still hadn't had a Pressure Relief Group or a spending plan. I still didn't sleep well: I had accrued an IRS debt while working at the paper, and I hadn't filed a return for two years. I still had not talked to my student loan officers, who were getting impatient.

A few months later, I found a job with the county with good benefits (previously I had had none) and higher pay. Just before I started, I convinced my sponsor she should give me a "not-quite-Pressure Relief Group," so I could go over my very first spending plan with her. She reluctantly agreed, telling me that it would be a one-shot deal—after that I would need to get my own Pressure Relief Group.

So now after over a year and a half in the program, I had a spending plan. Shortly after, I had my first real Pressure Relief Group. I contacted my creditors for temporary abeyances until I could get my act together. To my surprise, most creditors were happy to work with me. The ones who weren't were at least grudgingly willing. I filed my taxes with the help of a friend and began sending the IRS and the state a small good faith amount. I was able to answer my phone as well as open my mail.

A year later, with the support of my Higher Power, my Pressure Relief Group, and the meeting as a whole, I initiated a reclassification process of my job with the county. The process was frightening, long, and rigorous, but I stayed with it, sharing in meetings, praying, and making phone calls. My result was a substantial raise, including six months of back pay. My new job description was now congruent with what I was doing, and I saw hope for my career.

I used that back pay as down payment on my first car, paid off one student loan, and increased the amount I was paying the IRS.

I had never set up a formal agreement with the IRS, because my small payment hadn't even covered the interest and fines. Though I had been in great fear of the IRS, when I got the raise, I called them. It was a great relief to discover that they were surprisingly helpful. With my blessing, we set up a plan to take very reasonable payments out of my paycheck. A year later, difficulties in getting an apartment brought to light an IRS lien against my property. I satisfied the lien with a loan I will pay off in a year.

The state tax department never did set up an agreement with me. I sent them my small payment each month, gradually whittling away at the debt, with only an occasional dunning notice. When state policy changed and the dunning notices got uglier, the balance was small enough that I used part of my first IRS refund to pay it off.

My recovery is not a steady climb up a gentle hill; I backslide all over the place. It's hard for me to keep the records, and every six months or so, I miss a few weeks. I still bounce a check occasionally, although it's usually because of my math errors now. I still dig in my heels though, resisting and rebelling.

One thing I have learned is that I don't do anything until I am good and ready. With five years of recovery, working the Steps, and praying for willingness, I am good and ready faster, but just as resistant and stubborn on the way as I ever was. I do think I am more polite about it now. I have learned I can say that I am not ready for suggestions; when I *am* ready, I can ask for help then. I haven't blown my only chance. I am allowed to recover at my own pace, make my own mistakes, and try it my way first.

Even with all my resistance and rebellion, I keep coming back to D.A. My recovery continues. I look forward to my mail. I answer my phone. My debts are current. I no longer feel like a failure as an adult. I sleep nights now, even when I have slipped. I know that if a check bounces, I am not an evil person or an ugly human being. It means I am flawed, as we all are, and that I will have amends to make. Maybe it will be a fine, a trip back to the store if the bank didn't cover, a session with the bankbook to find the problem. It may mean that I need to look at the thinking behind the slip or error, that I need to make a phone call, do an inventory, or spend some time in meditation and prayer. I may need to reevaluate my behavior. But I do not need to doubt my worth as a person.

I Belong - An Underearner's Story

Meetings and Pressure Relief Groups gave the support needed to start a business, increase earnings, and commit to creative expression.

I believed I didn't belong in my first D.A. meeting. Few of the readings applied to me. I'm not in debt, and I don't compulsively spend money. If anything, I'm an underspender. I go on vacations and come back with half the money I took along. I rarely borrow money or anything else from friends. D.A. just didn't seem to apply to me.

I didn't return for a few months, but I finally reached a point of hopelessness and despair over my money situation and went again to D.A. This time I noticed that people at the meetings were discussing issues that did apply to me. As I began to work the program, I decided to practice the Twelve Step concept of 'take what you like and leave the rest.' I have now been attending D.A. for almost a year. Already my job, money and time issues have improved immeasurably. I mention these three areas of my life, because D.A. deals with more than financial debt.

My parents raised their children to live simply, not materialistically. Their beliefs sprung ostensibly from religious sources, but I now see my parents were conditioned by their background of scarcity: My mother was from a poor family; my father's father lived in a continuous state of money fear. Though I still believe in simple living, I now distinguish between not being materialistic and living in deprivation. For years I bought second-hand clothing. When I first got contact lenses, I felt so much guilt over my frivolous spending that I went back to glasses soon after.

My fear of spending money seemed to be realistic, because I rarely had enough money to live comfortably. For years I worked at one low paying job after another, alternating with going to school. At one time, even with my two Masters degrees, I earned $19,000 a year, a salary that barely covered living expenses in the expensive city where I lived. Only once did I have a well-paying job, but it was a job where I was unhappy. After quitting, I ended up doing many miserable temp jobs, collecting unemployment when those didn't pan out.

Once I got into D.A., I learned that money is a part of life, and that it's okay to map out how much I need and plan strategies for earning it. During my last Pressure Relief Group, I handed my spending chart for November and December to the group and waited for them to tell me I had to cut down on my spending. Instead, they said I didn't need to cut down—I needed to earn more and spend more. I looked back over my spending and realized I hadn't even allowed for necessities, such as shoes that fit properly. I am now earning a good hourly rate in a career that suits me and working on getting enough new clients to meet my spending and saving needs. In D.A., I've learned it's okay to be concerned with money.

Somehow I ended up with a lot of strange attitudes about work. I believed that work meant suffering and anxiety, and if something came easily to me it must be wrong. It never occurred to me that I could find work which paid a decent wage.

When I started working the D.A. program, I was doing work I hated. Because I wanted time in my life for creative activity I cared about, I was frustrated. I couldn't see a way out. It seemed like it was either/or. Either I spent all my time doing work I hated and had enough money to just barely live, or I had time for my art, but no money. Society's attitudes reflected this idea. Whenever I complained, people would say, "That's life. You have to be practical." Luckily, in D.A. I heard different. People there talked about right livelihood and *choosing* how to spend their time. I began to look at things I could do to earn a living that would also give me time for creativity.

Over a period of months, I decided on a possible career which would require running my own business. My worst enemy was the critic in my head who kept saying, "You're wasting your time. This will never get anywhere." By this time I had become so demoralized that I couldn't believe I would ever earn enough to live on again. Since I was starting my business in the middle of a recession, my critic seemed to be telling the truth. D.A. members countered these thoughts with their spirituality. They assured me that setting my mind on what I wanted and trusting a Higher Power was stronger than the recession. I realized that as long as my fear was holding me back from a commitment, I would not succeed. I set about starting my business and letting go of the results.

Though I am still building my business, I am earning more each month. Thanks to D.A.'s support, I am now doing work that I enjoy and that pays well.

I still get discouraged at times, but I am meditating and learning to trust in a Higher Power to determine the results. I've found it's okay to like my work.

As a child I spent a lot of time writing stories. As an adult, I never seemed to find the time. I was always saying to friends, "One of these days I'm going to put some time into writing." Whenever I thought about setting the time aside, however, I decided it was foolish, and I probably didn't have enough talent to get published. Every now and then I felt the urge to write, but I was always too busy doing more urgent things like finishing school, getting work done, or cleaning the bathroom.

D.A. encouraged me to make creative activity a priority and to stop thinking about the results in this area, too. I now take an acting class, and I write and perform my own material. I try not to focus on where this will go. It's likely my performances will never make me famous, but is that a reason to quit? Earlier I would have said yes, but I now believe in creativity for its own sake. Because I am self-employed, I can choose to set time aside for writing.

I see my time boundaries have never been strong. I used to come home and immediately answer every phone message on my machine, so my evenings were taken up by phone calls. And I ping-ponged back and forth between getting nothing done and trying to do everything at once. I would attempt to do the laundry, answer three letters, clean the apartment, go grocery shopping, make ten marketing calls, write a proposal, and meet a friend for dinner—all in one day. I believe this frantic activity comes from the sense of scarcity and deprivation I experienced around money matters. I do not believe there is enough time. Rushing around is a sign I believe *I* am in charge rather than a Higher Power.

Higher Power is the key to how D.A. works. As I struggle to remain hopeful, to build my business, and do my creative work, I need D.A. to remind me over and over that I can trust in something higher than myself. My mind tells me I have to worry and push constantly—that letting go even a little will result in disaster. My mind also tells me I have never done enough, that no matter what decisions I make, they will be wrong. Pretty discouraging.

Fortunately, I go to D.A. meetings to realize that a Higher Power exists and that I don't need a scarcity mentality. Whenever I replace scarcity with abundance in my thinking, I start to live in the moment, at a reasonable pace, without excessive anxiety. As my sponsor tells me, there is enough money, enough time, and enough love.

Finding My Own Voice

She agreed with her parents that she was wrong, especially about money.
In D.A., she learned to make her own decisions.

I am a recovering underearner and incest survivor. My difficulties dealing with money, food and relationships are the debilitating consequences of incest in my childhood. I believe there is hope, help, and a way to get through this, one day at a time, with the help of my Higher Power and by using the tools and Steps of D.A.

I am an only child who grew up in a prosperous area in the Midwest. My parents were professionals who regularly got raises and promotions. They had no problem with debt.

As an incest survivor I learned not to talk about what was really going on. It appeared my parents had money, but I never really knew. From the time I was very young until I came into D.A., I was in constant anxiety and confusion over how much my parents really did or did not have, and whether it was wrong to ask for things I needed. I always felt that something was wrong with me and that I would never make enough money to take care of myself because I was so extravagant. It would take weeks for me to ask for what I wanted. Sometimes I got what I asked for, but emotional pride was very high. The messages were: "We are hurting a lot because we have given this to you. We don't know what is the matter with you. You can't be trusted with money, so we will do it for you. We suffer because you have needs. You can't leave us, because we need you to take care of us. Anything you get you have to work very hard for, but then you have to give it to others less fortunate."

These messages taught me it was better to be vague and uncertain about what I really needed.

When I was in high school I used babysitting earnings to buy material to sew a skirt without telling my folks. They yelled and berated me for being extravagant and "bad." I really felt I had done something bad; there was something wrong with me. I put the material away until I was in college, away from my parents. This incident was confirmation that I couldn't make a "right" decision about money.

I also made "wrong" decisions about food. We often ate out in restaurants, and my father would make a scene over the cost. I learned to pick the cheapest thing on the menu, even if I wanted something healthier. Today I know the most abundant and loving thing to do is spend what it costs to have foods which are appropriate for me.

During my twenties and thirties, I would ask my parents for small amounts of money to tide me over when I wasn't working. It would take weeks for me to gather the courage. I would ask others if they thought it was okay for me to do this. Of course, everyone I asked had different opinions. Some people got money from their parents, no big deal. Others proudly never took a penny.

With the aid of Pressure Relief Groups and relying on my Higher Power, I can accept how much I really spend each month. I developed an ideal spending plan which puts my needs first. With the help of my Higher Power, I gradually let go of my fear of spending money on what I need and want. Making the ideal spending plan has given me an idea of how much I need to earn. When I identify, accept, and plan for my needs, I am serene.

For me, money creates the power to make choices for myself about what is the best way to meet my needs and wants. As an incest survivor, my recovery will destroy the old messages that I can't make my own decisions about what is best for me, or that I must always take care of someone else. By practicing the Sixth and Seventh Steps and praying, I ask my Higher Power to help me let go of the fear of leaving my family emotionally. This fear has lifted, as I now tell my family exactly what I need. As I practice the Eleventh Step of conscious contact daily and attend meetings regularly, my source of strength and serenity is not my parents, but my Higher Power.

The Gift of Awareness

*Though she drove into D.A. with a negative net worth
and a bad car loan, she found miracles.*

My compulsive debting dates back to getting my first credit card. My first year in graduate school was also my first experience of supporting myself through my own contributions. Although my salary was $411 a month, I saved $1,786 in ten months—enough to buy my first car. Then I got my first credit card, because I heard you needed it to establish a credit rating. I began with a $100 credit limit. Ten years later, I had four credit cards maxed out to $6,000 of unsecured debt. Interesting, how that happened. Every year around Christmas, I could count on a $200 raise in credit limit from at least one credit card. Each time, I'd swear up and down that I wouldn't use the credit, but I was always maxed out again by the next April. I always got a "raise" from the credit card companies, because I made debt repayment Number One on my priority list. If it came to a choice between going to the dentist or keeping current with my credit cards, guess which one I chose?

Because I was never hounded by irate creditors, it was easy for me to deny a problem. The issue that bottomed me out was an open-end car lease I took on when I got my first "real" job out of graduate school. The car had to be worth a given amount at the end of the lease. If it wasn't, I would make up the difference. I felt uneasy about entering the lease, because I worried that I couldn't take good enough care of the car for it to be at the desired value at the end of the lease. The the car wasn't even what I wanted. I was taking over a lease on a car with 15,000 miles on it. My boyfriend had set the deal up through a buddy. All my instincts told me to wait for a better deal. But in the spirit of "terminal vagueness" that typifies my compulsive debting, I signed the lease contract anyway.

My instincts proved to be right. I discovered my lease had all the disadvantages of actual car ownership with none of the advantages. I discovered that to renew the car registration, I had to pay an old parking ticket from the previous lessor. The car also had "little" things wrong: doors that wouldn't unlock, the rear trunk lid flew open without warning, and numerous other problems. I was determined to get rid of the car at the lease end, but was worried sick it wouldn't be worth its true value.

About a year into the lease, I started recovering in Overeaters Anonymous. Six months into my O.A. recovery, however, I started noticing things about my spending. I realized that though my salary was a lot bigger than in graduate school, I still didn't have enough money. A brochure from a bank showed how to calculate net worth, and to my dismay, mine was negative! The outcome of the car lease threatened to take my net worth even further down. What was wrong?

As the end of the lease drew near, I told my O.A. sponsor my fears of owing more to the leasing company than I could pay. She told me about Debtors Anonymous and referred me to a woman who took me to my first D.A. meeting. At first I wasn't sure whether I qualified. After all, I thought, I can pay my bills, so do I really belong with all those people who couldn't? But I was so scared about that lease I stayed and did everything they told me.

I started writing my money down and had a Pressure Relief Meeting after three months. One member of my Pressure Relief Group pointed out that for the monthly $200 I was paying for the leased car, I could have had a brand-new car. I was very angry, because I felt I'd been taken advantage of. My anger inspired me to do the right thing in the wrong way: Without consulting my Pressure Relief Group, I bought a new car using the leased car as the trade-in. Typically, I did not get clarity on the value of the leased car before I bought the new one. It was a big surprise the next month when a letter from the leasing company informed me that the discrepancy between what the car was supposed to be worth and how they valued it was $2,348! After reading that letter, I got down on my knees and prayed. With the help of my Pressure Relief Group, I negotiated a settlement for $1,100 that I was able to pay off—in cash—only nine months after my first D.A. meeting. How did this miracle happen, when I'd never had more than a hundred or two in savings? I'm not sure. In D.A., all I did was write my money down and not debt, one day at a time. Suddenly, I had money in the bank.

That was the first miracle that Debtors Anonymous worked in my life. I'm very grateful to D.A. and to my Higher Power for extracting me from the mess I'd gotten myself into. The biggest difference in my life since then is that I've been able to use the tool of awareness so that I can avoid situations like the car lease in the first place.

You don't hear much about awareness in D.A., so I'd like to make a pitch for it here. If you've ever read the A.A. Big Book, you may be familiar with the chapter called "More About Alcoholism." That chapter gives many examples of "alcoholic thinking," that is, the lame excuses that alcoholics give for drinking. The only freedom from alcoholic thinking must come from a Higher Power. As a compulsive debtor, I identified with the "alcoholic thinking" in my own disease, because I saw that "debting thinking" got me into the car lease mess. My main defense against "debting thinking" has been awareness. For me, awareness is not just a tool of the D.A. program; I see it as both a tool and a result of working the Twelve Steps—a gift from my Higher Power. Awareness is that little voice from my Higher Power that counteracts "debting thinking." Two examples from my later D.A. recovery illustrate this:

I signed up for a ballroom dance class with a famous dance studio. After I completed my first six lessons, I wanted to take more. However, the dance studio kept pressuring me to sign up for $3,200 worth of lessons "on time." Because of the gift of awareness, the unsecured debt immediately raised a red flag. I resisted their efforts to get me to sign up for a large number of lessons and arranged to take lessons on a pay-as-you-go basis. After taking a few lessons that way, I realized I wasn't making any progress. They wouldn't accommodate my needs; they wanted to pressure me into all the lessons at once and then map out a program for me. As weeks went by, I realized too that most people weren't there to learn how to dance. It was more of a social club. So, I quit.

I admit I didn't do this perfectly. The "Love Myself" savings fund suggested by my Pressure Relief Group was $800 poorer. I probably would have spent even less of my fund if I'd kept in better contact with my Pressure Relief Group. However, the gift of awareness undoubtedly saved me from incurring $3,200 in unsecured debt. In that sense, the $800 was money well spent. Progress, not perfection.

With the support of my Pressure Relief Group, I asked my credit card companies to cancel my line of credit. I could no longer use the cards, but I still received monthly statements and made payments. About a year later, a letter from one credit card company offered $5 if I reopened my line of credit. My debting mentality jumped at the thought: "Wow! Sounds like an easy $5. They must be counting on my using the credit line so they can get the interest, but if

I just reactivate the account without charging, I'll get the $5." I felt a funny twinge of awareness: I racked my brain trying to figure out why the bank would want to give me $5. I soon realized it was the $18 annual service fee. I'd be incurring $13 in unsecured debt: the $18 service fee minus the $5 for reactivating my account. Bully for awareness for warning me. This time around took only fifteen minutes to see the "catch."

This all shows me that just because I've paid off my debts doesn't mean I'm "cured." I'll always need awareness, the gift from my Higher Power, to protect me from making financial decisions not in my best interest.

Scarlett Comes Home To D.A.

A drama queen took it to the limit and found Higher Power.

I spent my entire life living beyond my means. As I child I had dreamed of a Scarlett O'Hara-like existence. As an adult I tried to make this dream a reality. I employed cleaning ladies, serving women for parties, housekeepers and nannies. I served the best food and liquor money could buy. I shopped at the most expensive stores for my children's clothes and mine and vacationed around the world. How could I do this on my husband's construction worker salary you ask? It was easy: Beg, borrow or steal. And when that didn't work, there were always credit cards. My theme song was "Take me to the limit one more time." I managed to squander both my husband's and my salary on looking good, but it wasn't long before all my money and marriage were "Gone With The Wind."

After leaving my family and moving to California, I was faced with the truth. I was a debtor, a pauper, and an underachiever. Oh, don't get me wrong. I could make lots of money, but I couldn't hold on to it. My family stopped bailing me out when time after time I ran another credit card to the limit. I came to a crashing halt. I had to live within my means. There was no place else to turn. Depression and suicidal thoughts were with me constantly. Now my bills were double my earnings, and I realized I would soon be living on the street.

Though I didn't know about D.A., I did start working the Steps in another program. Many people were encouraging me to go on social security, because I could barely work. I decided to try to support myself as best I could. It was the first time I had taken responsibility for myself, and it felt good. As part of my Fourth Step, I did financial amends, paying off all my credit cards and most of my debts. I was earning more money, and I had the feeling I could conquer the world.

That summer my uncle died, and I was left a large sum of money. I was made trustee for my children's and my widowed aunt's money. It was money, money, money that brought me to D.A. six months later. I was again depressed, suicidal, and hysterical. I felt totally responsible and afraid I would make a mistake and lose all the money. I tried to hide, manipulate and control everyone's funds. I got greedy and wanted more, so I would feel secure. But no matter how I hoarded, counted or concealed it, there just was not enough. I look back on these months as my Silas Marner period. I had no life, no God—just money. My relationship with my children was based on money. It was all we talked about: They asked for it, and I was the "Almighty" that decided whether they could have it. I was sick, hysterical and unsure of my life, but completely in control of theirs. How could this be happening when I had worked the Steps and was in a Twelve Step program for over ten years?

On New Year's Day eight years ago, I joined D.A. I went to a meeting every week. I set up a Pressure Relief Group immediately and have met with the same two people almost every month since joining D.A. Thanks to the commitment of this man and woman, I have lost many of my fears. I have gone from boxes of bills, papers and twelve bankbooks to one Higher Power. I went from depending on my will to surrendering to God's. One of the most difficult issues I faced was using money from savings for my everyday life. Every time I dipped into savings for food and shelter, I faced my deprivation issues. I wanted to save the money or hide it, but never to spend it. I was afraid if I spent it, there wouldn't be enough. Some people in the program think their problems would be solved by a certain sum of money. I have not found that to be true. Even today, I call on my Higher Power when using prudent reserve funds or savings. I remind myself that there is enough. I am being taken care of by my H.P.

Money is no longer my god. I turned my children's money over to them after educating them on how to manage it. They make mistakes, but that's how they learn. I trust that they have an H.P. too. My relationship is clear with all in my family, thanks to D.A. I have learned money is only a tool. I am financially solvent and earn more now than in the past seven years. The most important thing I have received from D.A. is the personal relationship I have with my Higher Power. All the meetings, literature, phone calls, Pressure Relief Groups, and sponsors have only one purpose: to help you and me find God. My H.P. is right here when I am in need. No matter how much or how little money I have, I'm okay. I have enough, because I am enough. Thanks to D.A., I don't have to cling to the mud of Tara to keep me safe. I am at home, no matter where I am. D.A. is my home.

Mario's Story

Hopeless with money, he became willing to accept help. With the support of the fellowship, he stayed solvent throughout his fatal illness.

This year, I celebrate four years of recovery in Debtors Anonymous. Five years ago, I decided that the reason I felt so hopeless around money was that I hadn't applied myself. Well, after one year of applying my self-knowledge, I was even more hopeless than when I began. I was ready for help. Now I was teachable, and my Higher Power brought me to my first D.A. meeting. I had many years' experience in other Twelve Step programs, so it was a little easier to fit in. Still, I walked in with much fear, shame, and confusion about my finances. My love interest had been going to D.A. for a year, and his life seemed to be improving, especially around his finances. He didn't once suggest I go to D.A., but as the program says, it is attraction rather than promotion.

Well, it worked. My partner drove helpless me to my first D.A. meeting on a bleak December Sunday, and I'll always be grateful for the principles of Debtors Anonymous. I hated my first year of meetings, but I knew I was in the right place. I kept coming back.

I've never had open-heart surgery, but I think I now know what it feels like. When other members shared about not being able to buy underwear, not opening mail, feeling like there wasn't enough, like they weren't enough, not knowing how to deal with creditors, I felt I wasn't alone. That feeling of hopelessness I had learned to accommodate was lifted at my first meeting and has not returned. That's one of the most precious gifts I've received from D.A.

A lot of my recovery has focused on the fact that I live with another life-threatening disease besides debting, though I have seen debting kill people as cunningly as drugs or alcohol. I am a recovering debtor who is living with AIDS. As my recovery progresses, so does the AIDS virus. I'm learning that just as I am powerless over debting and cannot recover alone, neither can I deal with AIDS by myself. As an active debtor, I became isolated and secretive. So it's a miracle of

D.A. that last night I had a D.A. meeting in my home with an oxygen tube in my nose and six other D.A. members who have helped me in more ways than they'll ever know. I hope I've helped them; that's how it works!

When I came to D.A., I knew I had to eventually do service, if I were going to stay. I made coffee, became the literature person, gave my phone number to newcomers (even though I felt I had nothing to offer), gave and received Pressure Relief Groups, and became a part of Intergroup. The effort I've put into my program has come back to me tenfold in the way of friendships, serenity, self-esteem, and self-love.

One painful and joyful lesson I keep learning in D.A. is that I have needs, and they all deserve to be met. As I grew up in a family of debtors, having a need was just unheard of. As a debtor living, and I emphasize living, with AIDS, I have many needs. When my virus is causing me to feel sick, my first instinct is to hoard all my resources and shut down. That is my disease rearing its ugly head. I've tasted enough abundance to not stay there for very long, and I actively use the tools of D.A. That's a miracle—getting out of being stuck, shut down. That was how I lived 24 hours a day, before D.A.

Because of the Twelve Steps and principles of D.A. and its loving members, I've maintained my health insurance, stayed solvent even with my medical bills, and received massages, affection and physical and emotional support. I feel loved and supported by my Higher Power and all of my needs are being met. I'm able to open my mail daily. I'm in a loving relationship with the debtor who Twelve Stepped me—we just celebrated six years. I pay for my therapy weekly, and I could go on and on. You get the picture though.

I have not had a perfect recovery, although I would like to. My smart-mouthed therapist referred to me as "little Ghandi." Okay, I get it! I have not had a formal sponsor for two years, and I don't think I've ever completed any of my Action Plans, and I've not been treasurer, but this is all okay; I am enough.

Especially to anyone new to D.A.: I hope I've given you a message of hope. I've learned through D.A. that no suffering member is hopeless—I'm proof of that.

When I came to D.A. in December, I didn't have enough money to buy a gift. As I celebrate my fourth year in D.A., I just made a list of presents I'm buying (my name is at the top), and we are planning a Christmas party that's within each other's spending plan. The best present I get every December is that I am a member of Debtors Anonymous.

Publisher's Note: This member died on December 4, 1992.

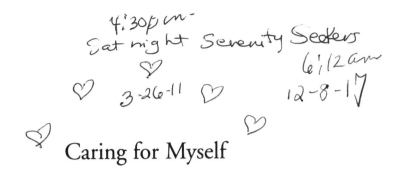

4:30pm -
Sat night Serenity Seekers
6:12am
3-26-11 ♡ 12-8-17
♡ ♡ ♡

Caring for Myself

Though his early family experiences taught him shame,
he learned to value himself in D.A.

As a recovering member of Debtors Anonymous for over five years, I have achieved clarity about what it means to care for myself. In D.A., I have learned to sort through the various manifestations of the disease and to identify with others. Although my story is simple, it also reveals ways of manifesting the disease of compulsive debting which I thought of as unique to me.

My first debt was to my parents, and I incurred it when I was only seven or eight years old. I received an allowance, and I was supposed to set a portion aside to pay for school supplies in September. Being a kid, however, what I really wanted was to buy baseball cards, like the other boys could. When school started, I had no money for pencils and notebooks.

My mother and I made an agreement that, instead of receiving a nickel for drying the dinner dishes, that money would be used to pay down my debt. I can still remember the shame I felt and the fear I had that this debt would *never* be paid off. I had the sense that I could not hold my head up as long as I owed that money.

Years later, I've come to see that, while it was simply my parents' intention to teach me responsibility about money, I was too young for such a lesson. What I took away from that experience instead was a sense that I was incapable of managing money or of supporting myself.

Over the years, I lived with my sense of inadequacy. Although my background was comfortably middle-class and we didn't lack anything material, even with my parents' conservative tastes, I lived in fear of being without income.

Despite my fears of not being able to take care of myself, I acquired a profession and a career in civil service. Having grown up New York City, I took advantage of my new status to relocate, first to Washington, D.C., then to San Francisco.

I started to acquire credit cards and with each, soon charged up to the limit. I would go into a panic and focus all my effort toward paying them off as quickly as possible to avoid the shame of my childhood debting experiences. In keeping with that, I put the needs of my creditors before my own, reinforcing the idea that I needed to pay them off to be an acceptable human being.

I came to my first D.A. meeting more than ten years ago. At that time, I was earning more money than I ever had before. Yet each week my money dwindled away more quickly. I had recently returned to San Francisco from a trip to a wedding on the East Coast. Transportation, lodging, and the wedding gift I charged to my credit card, because I didn't have any cash. Shortly after moving to San Francisco, I had purchased a late-model used car and had left all the details of financing and insurance up to the car dealer. I was vague about what it would cost me for loan payments and insurance, and since I hadn't planned on buying a car, I hadn't allowed for the expense of keeping it. Nor had I found a place to live where I could park a car off-street. I found myself paying, in addition to my rent, a monthly fee for garage space.

In order to generate enough cash for all these unplanned expenses, I purposely had an inadequate amount of money withheld from my paycheck for income taxes. I had no idea what I would do when the time came the following year.

By the time I reached D.A., I had cleaned up other areas of my life in other Twelve Step programs. I knew the Steps worked, but I couldn't conceive of how to apply them to my money problems. What I did know was that I couldn't control my situation. While my debts were relatively modest in dollars compared to some of the stories I heard in my early meetings, they were more than I could deal with on my own.

I went to meetings, listened, and told my new friends in D.A. what was going on with me. Despite my fears of disclosing my financial situation to others, I quickly assembled a Pressure Relief Group. My previous money difficulties and my acquaintance with some of the early D.A. members in Washington, D.C. had motivated me to start keeping spending records.

My Pressure Relief Group showed me I could make sound choices in order to get my needs met. They assured me that, if I wanted to, I could keep my car. They worked with me while I searched for a new apartment which would meet my needs better and still cost a great deal less than the previous one. They held my hand as I got clarity about my tax situation. Later on, my Pressure Relief

Group and my other D.A. friends supported me in the painful process of dealing with my debt to the IRS. The job I moved to San Francisco to take was not suited for me. Working the Third Step, I requested reassignment and was able to stay in the same office, with no decrease in pay.

My recovery in D.A. helped me to form and maintain an abundant and rewarding relationship with a loving partner, who followed me into D.A. (and whose story also appears in these pages). As I write these words, I mourn his passing from AIDS, an event which happened just a few weeks ago. Thanks to this program working in both our lives, we were able to share a beautiful home for the final two years of his life. Each of us, with the help and support of our program, was able to plan vacations beyond what we ever could have conceived prior to recovery—all paid for, in cash, without depriving ourselves in other areas.

It is a tribute to this D.A. recovery that my partner had adequate medical care, and there was no financial crisis after he died. It is a signpost of my recovery that I could have provided financial support, if it had been necessary. In addition, during the process of his dying, it was important that I get my needs met so that I could be there for him. It took all the resources I could muster from my recovery to ask for help, to ask for time away from him, to allow myself opportunities for fun and recreation so that I could be emotionally available for him and for myself.

It is hard to conceive of anything more painful than the loss of a loved one from a terminal illness. I know that I too am at risk for AIDS, and this fact is an important part of my D.A. program. It means that health care is a high priority in my spending plan; my physical, spiritual, and emotional well-being come first in my life. It also gives me the humility I need to live my life one day at a time.

I've long since paid off my unsecured debts, including my debt to the IRS. Those were the debts that brought me to my knees and brought me to the rooms of Debtors Anonymous. Even my car loan has been paid off. The money my Higher Power brings into my life is mine to use as I see fit: to meet all of my needs and many of my desires, to contribute to the causes I care about, and to give myself a prudent reserve.

As I look to the future, I know that my continued well-being depends upon my willingness to continue to reach out for support and for love. First and foremost, I must ask for the help of my Higher Power on a daily basis.

3-26-11

keys

That spiritual support is, after all, the very foundation of the D.A. program. In addition, I have always to reach out to my friends in D.A. and to all of the resources which I am now able to believe I deserve. I am worthy.

Bridges to Cross and Worlds to Conquer

Shopping was safe at first, but it led to debt, anxiety, emptiness, and eventually D.A.

There is a story behind every story. Mine begins in the city of Los Angeles, California, what is now called South Central Los Angeles. As far back as I can remember, I have escaped to the world of shopping, grazing and inventorying. At the age of five this was spurred on by scenes of rage, lack, poverty and isolation. Money was always an issue with my family. Although the disease expressed itself in other media, this was a group and family experience. The experience was not to have and to always need. Waiting for the other shoe to drop in our home built enough anxiety and pressure in me that my first relief came from shopping and being alone in the supreme silence of myself. A melancholy, creative little introvert emerged who could make herself appear funny, happy-go-lucky and a giant among people. Thus the duality was born.

The local five-and-dime became my first step away from the reality of my life. I was just tall enough to see over the little glass dividers that held the merchandise. I could walk up and down the aisles of the store with my money clutched in my hand in a process of coveting, picking up and putting down each item. Then I would dissect my money a thousand ways, playing the game in my head: What would it feel like if I owned that particular thing? Turning off and shutting down my mind became a way of life. In time, other anesthesia developed including old movies, daydreaming, and reading. As an elementary and junior high school student, I could always figure out ways to make little shopping sprees: babysitting, odd jobs for family members, turning in soda water bottles for the refunds, and making friends with kids who had much more than I did. They could and would always be a source of generosity.

By the time I reached high school, I had a job at a clothing store where my paycheck never made it to the bank. The attraction to the path of acquiring, spending and compulsive-obsessive behavior was a powerful vehicle that remained the same for years. Fixing up the outside of myself became the ultimate obsession. It was clothes, shoes, accessories and things. The people that I could relate to were the ones with all style and no substance. I was driven toward the look-good victims.

In time I married a man who was bound for a life of success, money and prestige. What a wonderful way to conquer a hostile country, state, and city. This place and time was tamed by the colors gold and green—that is, the gold card and the greenback. During my marriage I became the proud parent of two children and earned a degree in Interior Design. Along with the newly acquired knowledge of fabric, I also became a seamstress and wearable artist. My closet was color coordinated, so that I could find out if there was a hole in my wardrobe that needed obsessing over. The child within perceived herself as still lacking while price tags remained on many of the clothes.

During the journey to success, we moved twenty-two times to as many homes in eight different states. The only consistency in my life was shopping and acquiring. I made all sales personnel into great one-dimensional relationships. Their only duties were to act as if they were glad to see me coming and to search for that ultimate purchase which would add to the color-coded closet. On this road to debting, spending and paupering, I also acquired the hobby habit: painting, collecting miniatures, dolls, teapots, kaleidoscopes, dishes, books, seminars, workshops and reading materials, just to name a few.

The irony of the hobby habit is that each element fueled the insanity of "more is not enough." Each category captivated my mind, body and soul. The laser beam focus absorbed everything; it felt like a black hole. I would reach a crescendo of debt, shame and remorse. The end result always led to panic, fear and insecurity while trying to get out of the cycle of debting and acquiring. After a bout like this, a brief reprieve would ensue, allowing me to graze, inventory and find another obsession. This pattern had eroded my spiritual life. I now understand that this process was my higher power since the age of five.

If it had not been for my descent into the depths of bills, credit cards and that powerlessness, I would not have found Debtors Anonymous. I had been in another Twelve Step program for ten years when I found D.A. For me this disease has always painted a perfect picture of hopelessness, despair, and a life less than bountiful. I have learned to love the idea that it takes what it takes to reach a bottom. The bottom, or end to this tunnel, became a loyal, tried and true friend. Reaching the bottom of any disease is essential. Coming to that point makes one open up to the loving, outstretched hands of a Higher Power, one I choose to call God. Those hands have broken my fall on many occasions, and each time the bottom has risen. Today I am grateful for the ascent. The process of climbing out of the shaft of debt has allowed me to take the time to heal and care for the bruises, scrapes, bumps, and gouges I incurred while active in the disease.

I have received a vision concerning my recovery in D.A. The vision is that the greatest of artists can only paint a picture one brushstroke at a time. The artist has to employ the elements and principles of design in order to have a successful painting. Some of the elements are balance, harmony, consistency, space, volume, texture and light, just to name a few. Searching and researching into the spiritual life is necessary to become effective in the business of living. No one else can be a stand-in for my role in life. I actually have to pick up the paints and brushes with my own hands and use the canvas that was given to me. In my recovery I have prayed for the courage to hold on to each fragment of myself and to have joy for each bit of progress that is proffered and taken to my spiritual bank. Looking back or quitting is not an option. This disease tells me that since I am not perfect in my program of action, I am not successful in my recovery. Instead of listening to the disease, I hold on to the fact that once my paintbrush has been put to the canvas, my stroke is excellent. This literally means that I have done my best.

The disease to this day is cunning, baffling and powerful. My claim and promise is that my Higher Power has given me the tools to prevail. A completed canvas is supported by an easel of grace that sustains me in every moment of powerlessness. Today in this arena of powerlessness, I am grateful to be in active recovery with the freedom and ability to paint the bridges to cross and the worlds to conquer.

Saved By a Power Greater Than Myself

*This member exchanged a career of debting
for a loan-free graduate education.*

I grew up in a middle-class suburban family that didn't seem all that different from the other families I knew. We didn't talk much about money. I never had an allowance and never really developed a good idea of the relationship between income and expenses.

One thing I do remember is that my parents used credit cards a lot—and for everything, including department store purchases, gasoline, and eating out. Naturally, I assumed that part of being an adult was being able to use plastic money. Little did I know how that attitude would start me on a reckless path of compulsive debting that I could never control.

I started getting credit when I was only 17, and therefore not even old enough to be legally responsible for my debts. By the time I was 20, I had at least a half dozen credit cards from various department stores and banks and hundreds of dollars of debt. Nevertheless, I really loved what I thought was the adult-like feeling that charging things gave me. It also was a nice way of saying to the world that I deserved respect, which was important since I had little inherent self-esteem.

For example, I usually traveled using an old backpack, wearing old blue jeans and a flannel shirt. I had a shaggy dark beard and hair over my collar. Looking like a cross between a hippie and a mass murderer, I would show up in airports and train stations with my backpack and slap my credit card down to pay for my ticket. It was a way of saying, "You may think I'm a bum, but you better respect me since I've got status!"

Once I was out of college and had a job, the credit card offers started rolling in; I accepted all of them, of course. I used credit cards to buy furniture and food, clothing and rental cars. When I got a 25% raise after six months, I figured that there was no reason to worry about debt. Inflation was in double digits, and I assumed that my income would continue to rise. The credit cards could get paid off later with deflated currency.

Two years of this and I had five bank cards, twice that many department store cards, and a new car that I had bought with $200 down, obtained, of course, via a credit card cash advance. My pattern was that I would buy on impulse, especially at sales. Nothing was ever planned, and so I never got anything that cost more than the amount of credit still available on my credit cards. I never really took any nice vacations, or got to see the world, or gave myself any other really nice things that I could remember—that would have taken planning.

The thing that saved me in those early years was that even though I would hit the limits, another creditor would offer me a new credit card or line of credit! Eventually though, the banks must have realized that I was in over my head and the new pre-approved cards stopped coming. I realized it too and saw my first credit counselor—fully six years before I discovered Debtors Anonymous.

The credit counselor did not understand what the problem was. I had a high income, a steady job, and the ability to add up the totals on a budget. She designed a budget for me and politely dismissed me from her office. Oh, if only it were so easy!

Merely using credit totally messed up my cash flow. My bank account was never an accurate reflection of how much money I had available, because I never knew how much money the creditors would ask for when that month's bills came due. Since I often exceeded the credit limits, the entire amount over the limit would need to be paid. I would borrow from one card to pay another. I also loved the "90 days same as cash" and "six months deferred billing" offers that some stores had. The entire situation was a morass of uncertainty.

I made things worse for myself by putting other people's interests before my own. I was active in politics and got on what seemed like every good cause mailing list that existed. I was a sucker for the mail order plea for money. And that misplaced generosity extended to my friends and family. One Christmas I pawned my stereo in order to purchase presents for others.

Then things got worse. I lost my job and got married in rapid succession. My wife did not mind me not having an income for a while, and her acceptance of my situation probably blinded me to things I should have noticed that were not working in the relationship. I guess I really needed affirmation. My employment had provided that; now that I was then unemployed, I guess I subconsciously hoped that a relationship could replace my nearly nonexistent self-esteem.

About this time two more credit counselors failed to get me to mend my ways. Debtors Anonymous was still four years away. Actually, in all fairness, the counselors had no idea that this disease really had very little to do with money. I really tried to follow their advice and their very restrictive budget. The deprivation from never being able to buy clothes or eat out was too much to take, however. I was working very hard at a well-paying job and seeing nothing from it. My pattern, repeated several times, was to keep the budget for a few months, then blow it all in one massive unplanned spending binge.

Not that this changed any of my ways! It was at about this time that my then-spouse and I purchased a condominium with no money down—the developer even lent us the money for the closing costs. I totaled my first car and the insurance money was insufficient to pay off the note and get a replacement, so I bought another car with an insufficient down payment. A fourth credit counselor failed to help.

Eventually, our marriage broke up and the expenses mounted up—attorneys, court costs, temporary living expenses. The good thing was that I got into a Twelve Step program to help me deal with my relationships. I was essentially homeless, moving from one friend's basement to another's living room.

One day I was in a recovery-oriented bookstore and saw a loose-leaf binder with information about lots of different Twelve Step programs. I leafed through page after page, reading about all kinds of fellowships to help people deal with powerlessness over all kinds of aspects of life—gambling, emotions, drugs, relationships, eating, sex. The Step Twelve advice to "practice these principles in all our affairs" really seemed to have been taken seriously, given the variety of affairs in which people seemed to be using the principles. Each page in the binder had several paragraphs about the particular fellowship, and contact information, both addresses and telephone numbers.

I then came upon an almost empty page. All it said was "Debtors Anonymous" and a telephone number. I had no idea what it was about, but I knew that nothing had ever worked for my spending and debting, and that I was willing to try anything. I copied down the telephone number and called as soon as I got home. A few days later I got a call from a member of D.A. who told me where and when the meetings in the area were held. I attended the first one I could, the first of many, over six years ago.

They told me there were three things I should do. First, I should stop incurring any additional unsecured debt. For me, that meant no more credit cards.

Well, I had done that for short periods in the past without any trouble—it was maintaining that abstinence for longer times that was the problem. Nevertheless, I said okay to that one. Second, I was told to come to six meetings in two weeks. I was lucky that there were four meetings each week within three miles of where I lived, and all were on the subway line.

The big problem was the third thing they told me to do. I was instructed to write down in a little notebook every penny I spent and every penny I earned. I had known people who had done this, and my evaluation of them was that they were obsessive control freaks. I had neither the desire nor interest in knowing in such detail what I was spending money on. Years later I can see that my real desire was to maintain my fog of vagueness over all my finances.

Nevertheless, I decided to give it a try. I had already tried four different private credit counselors and knew I couldn't handle this problem myself. I have to remind myself, when newcomers come to D.A. meetings who are reluctant to use the tools, that many of us must try all the self-will methods before fully admitting powerlessness. I had simply tried them before I had ever heard of Debtors Anonymous. If I had discovered D.A. six years earlier, I don't know whether or not I would have been willing to surrender to the program.

For me, perhaps even more important than the admission of my own powerlessness was that I met people who seemed to have solved their personal spending or debt crises through D.A. What was most striking to me was the number of people who were taking nice vacations—and not just a week at a nearby beach in a crowded run-down beach house! One person was about to go to Rio de Janeiro. Yet another was about to leave for a Caribbean cruise, another had just been to Switzerland and was about to go to Japan, and yet another was saving for a trip the following year to Hong Kong. And everyone was paying in cash! When they shared where they had been financially before D.A., I couldn't believe it. I became willing very quickly to act as if the power of this program could help me—even though it was some time before I really believed it.

About two months later I had my first Pressure Relief Meeting. I was the good little D.A.er and put all of my income and expense recording onto a computer spreadsheet. There was a good and a bad reason for doing this. The good reason is that I tend to sabotage myself with arithmetic errors—and I have a graduate degree in Applied Mathematics!

The bad reason is that I got a sense of power and control over the numbers by using a computer program. The truth is that the numbers recording income and expense are not there to run and control my life or for me to control or manipulate. The numbers just are. The numbers are just a statement of the truth as to what my values have been for the particular month. It would be some time before I really got this concept deep down. The spending plans I work out with my Pressure Relief Meetings are a prospective look at my values, and the records of what I spend are a retrospective look. When the actual expenditures differ greatly from what I had planned, it means that something is out of control or that I was not telling the truth in the first place about what I valued. And that is it—no judgments attached. I just need to look at why and how my actual spending differs from my plan so that I can correct the situation in the future.

Anyway, I took my eight-inch-high stack of computer printouts into my first Pressure Relief Meeting and the two members of my Pressure Relief Group refused to look at them! They said that I had too much attention on the numbers and not enough on the spiritual side of the program and of life. They had me talk for a long time about what I really wanted in life. Later, they had me make a list of things I wanted in life for myself. At that point, most of the things were material possessions or travel opportunities, since I had been feeling deprived for so long. The biggest ones were to own my own place, to live in a historic building, and to take a trip to Arizona to hike the Grand Canyon. I would learn later that these are examples of what some D.A.ers call visions, and that it is very important to keep these things in mind as we work the day-to-day program. We started on a spending plan that met all these ideals. We put dollar values by each item, but I was instructed not to total the items until the next Pressure Relief Meeting. I came out of that first Pressure Relief Meeting a bit surprised. A Pressure Relief Meeting where I wasn't pressured!

We did add up the numbers in the ideal spending plan at the second Pressure Relief Meeting, and I can see why they did not want me to add them up for myself. The monthly average total for that ideal spending plan was over $1,300 more than my income at the time. They explained to me that I could have anything on the list of ideals (visions) that I wanted, but that I had to plan and that I would not be able to have all of them at once. Well, I was willing to try that, since all of my own efforts had yielded none of them, ever.

A funny thing was happening to me as I continued attending meetings. The desire to use my credit cards disappeared. That first Christmas without debting was tight, but it was a real relief when January came around, and I knew I did not have to worry about surprises in the mail. I started to get a sense that I would get through all this. And I knew it was not me doing it alone. I had the program. I had a Power greater than myself.

Another thing my first Pressure Relief Meeting told me was that I should stop shopping for things on sale. Sales, I was told, encouraged compulsive spending. An amazing thing occurred. I didn't want to go to sales anymore. I was more interested in getting the things on my visions list than in whatever was on sale for what might be the last time. Planning for the larger visions was more important. For the first time, I had a sense that I might get some.

I was also told to stop giving so much to others. Giving is important in D.A.—it is important to feel enough prosperity that I can share it with others. However, what I was doing was giving at the expense of myself. One of the principles, I think, of this program is that there is always enough, and that there will *always* be enough, to go around. My Higher Power will see to it that my needs are taken care of as long as I continue to work the tools and Steps of this program. My spending plans, developed with my Pressure Relief Group through the inspiration of a Power Greater Than Me, reflect my values as to what I need and want at this time. I can share some of my prosperity—in both time and money—with others, but not at the expense of my own. That is one reason I contribute to the basket every single time it is passed at meetings and why I continue doing service work in my fellowship. I also contribute time and money to my church and occasionally to political candidates I support. But I don't feel that I have to give to every single good cause that finds a way to put my address on its mailing list.

And I have so often seen for myself the fact that there is always enough to go around for so many people that I cannot deny that fact anymore. I have sponsored or done Pressure Relief Groups for people in all walks of life. This includes D.A.ers who have been homeless or who have received public assistance as well as D.A.ers with high six-figure incomes. I have known D.A.ers who could not ever have another checking account or were in legal trouble because of their debts and D.A.ers who were hardly in debt at all, but felt equally out of control. Whatever my problems have been, there has been someone else whose problem, though different from my own, seems even more impossible (to me) to deal with. Nevertheless, that person's Higher Power gets him or her through the difficulties. The only way that I can screw this program up is to think that I've got it licked and don't need D.A. any more.

Within two years of entering D.A., I had started taking some vacations. I purchased a co-op apartment in a historic building with beautiful landscaping on the subway line—and with a real down payment. No more gimmick financing! I began to enjoy some of the endless prosperity that is available, even though I still owed debts. About a year into D.A., I started thinking about lifestyle issues. For example, was the career that was my source of income really rewarding?

About a year and a half into D.A., I really got serious about working the Steps and did my first D.A. Fourth Step. I guess I really didn't want to do it at first—I carried around the A.A. Big Book and an empty pad of paper for several weeks, hoping the inspiration would hit me to start writing. Finally, I was volunteering in the office at a folk festival, monitoring a telephone that nobody ever called, and I started writing to relieve the boredom.

I followed the resentments and fears format described in the Big Book. Lots of resentments came up—toward previous employers, toward schools I had attended, toward people who had lent me money, toward myself. Fears of financial uncertainty also came up. I really liked having a steady income, in what I thought were layoff-proof jobs. Yet, I had sacrificed a lot of my aliveness for security.

What I found was something I had known for a long time but had never admitted to myself. I felt a calling to teach at the university level. I had even taught part-time at a local community college, but to do any more than that required more education. I shared this with some of the local D.A. old timers in a Fifth Step, and they encouraged me to follow my dream. So with that I set out to investigate leaving my career and applying to full-time graduate school—at each step turning over the result to my Higher Power.

I contacted a former professor, who offered encouragement. I obtained the applications and filled them out—letting HP give me the words for the essay. I took the Graduate Record Exam in a roomful of people a decade younger than me—letting HP give me the answers—and did very well. I applied for admission and was accepted. I applied for financial aid and received a full scholarship toward a Ph.D. with the promise of part-time employment. And I took the risk and matriculated—even though I was still in debt. Perhaps most importantly, D.A. gave me the self-esteem to enter a challenging academic program and feel I was worthy of being successful. I've gone to professors' office hours without feeling intimidated. I take examinations expecting to do well. I do research expecting to find the answer.

I sold my co-op with a small profit and moved to a new city, with a new significant other. At the time I applied to that school, there was only one Debtors Anonymous meeting in that new city. I vowed to support the program that had so helped me and to trust my Higher Power to work things out. Today, four years later, there are nine D.A. meetings in the metropolitan area where I attend school.

My significant other and I were married a year into my graduate school. This required new levels of turning life over and even more commitment to work my D.A. program. We planned and had a prosperous wedding and honeymoon with the aid of our Pressure Relief Group and Higher Power. And I still owed debts.

Part of the point is that life does not have to stop until debts are paid. Debtors Anonymous is about living life prosperously one day at a time, regardless of one's financial situation. My debts were finally paid off two years into graduate school and four years into D.A., and there was not much of a difference in my life as a result. My spending plan changed, but my serenity and sense of worth did not. That is because through Debtors Anonymous I had learned that my prosperity, serenity, and spirituality were a function of how well I worked the Steps and tools, not a function of my bank balance. And this has continued through more recent trials and tribulations: my mother's illness and eventual death, qualifying exams, changing advisors. My concept of God, my Higher Power, keeps changing. Yet no matter how I define it, my Higher Power still seems to work for me and for everyone else I know who works the program.

Today I am in my fourth year of graduate school, writing my dissertation. I am living more prosperously with my graduate student research assistantship than I did in my pre-D.A. days with a yuppie income. Yet the material prosperity of this program is only a small part of recovery.

Through Debtors Anonymous I can deal with any situation, any upset, any problem. I know that with the aid of my Higher Power and my fellow members of D.A., there is no situation in the world than can possibly occur that cannot be handled in a way that my needs are met. This sense of security is not something anybody can take away from me. It is not dependent upon my bank balance, my employer, or any one other individual besides me. It is a sense of security with a drive for control. I can take risks that I once thought were not possible. And even when I screw things up, I can work Step Ten, clean up the mess I made, and rediscover the serenity and peace of this program at once. I can honestly say this program is more valuable than any amount of money in the world.

The Diamond-Covered Dress

This member needed to know if she could trust God, so she tested him, again and again. In D.A. she found that God helped her trust herself.

By the time I was born, the youngest girl with three older brothers, it was pretty obvious that my father had a problem with alcohol. His compulsive behavior spilled over into many areas: spending, debting, and overeating. I remember my mom fretting about the way my dad spent money. No sooner had she paid off the debts than he would have the family back in debt again.

Supposedly, to the outside world we looked great. We were affluent, well-educated, and living in a beautiful seventeen-bedroom, four-bathroom beach-front home in Hawaii. My parents were well-known and highly accomplished people in the community. At the height of my father's alcoholism, when he was having four-day blackouts, he was president of a national organization, deacon and co-founder of our church, and a successful businessman. My mom was also a successful professional in her own right.

On the inside though, our family was very sick. My father reached the point where he had to have a drink almost around the clock. He was a very belligerent drunk, verbally abusing the kids constantly with put-downs. My mom's highly successful and demanding career caused her to be gone a lot, and my father would promise not to drink during her absence. From what I remember, he got drunk every time she left.

One Saturday, we woke up to find my father drunk at 8:00 in the morning. This morning was a turning point for our family. My mom gave him a choice: Stop drinking or leave. I remember going into the living room feeling very detached. I told my dad he had a choice, the family or the bottle. I could see that he was powerless over alcohol and that he was sick. I felt detached because there was nothing I could do. He had to reach out for help.

As a child, I was deprived of feelings, warmth, comfort, safety and unconditional love. No one talked about what was going on, and I learned at an early age that it was not safe to share my feelings. Around age six, I found comfort in taking things that did not belong to me: stealing. When we would go on trips and visit people, I would steal knickknacks from coffee tables and bookshelves. I just had to have those pretty things.

I was feeling alone and overwhelmed by the emotional deprivation in our family, and there wasn't anyone safe to talk to. I decided to test God to see if He really existed and was the great and omnipotent Being the church made Him out to be. I asked Him for a sign of His existence. It would have to be something foolproof, leaving no doubt in my little six-year-old mind. I asked for a diamond-covered dress.

A few weeks later, we went on a family trip to Chicago. At dinner with my parents and their friends, the woman turned to me and said, "I have something I want to give you that I know you will really like." She left the room, shortly returning with a dress completely covered with "diamonds." Her daughter was an Olympic ice-skating champion, and this dress had been a costume for the competition. It was a short dress on her daughter, but on me, at age six, it was a full-length dress.

When I was twelve years old, something critical happened. I suppressed the memory of it until later in my adult life. This incident placed me in solid agreement with my father: I was not deserving of respect. It was then that I committed myself to deprivation, the belief that I was not enough and did not deserve abundance in my life. I was approached sexually by a man and ran to my father for protection. Instead of protection, I was met with harsh interrogation and anger. I felt so much shame that I believed my father was right—I was not okay and didn't deserve anything good. I made a silent promise not to feel. Nothing was ever discussed about this incident in the days following, and I stuffed the whole experience away, deep inside.

Very soon after though, my father miraculously sobered up in Alcoholics Anonymous. We moved out of the beautiful beach house into a little three-bedroom apartment in the city, leaving the affluent life behind for a new spiritual life. I saw it as a choice between the affluent lifestyle of the beach house and my dad's recovery. This was a logical connection between the affluent life we had and the cause of my father's alcoholism, which had devastated my life. I was willing to give up affluence to attend open A.A. meetings with my dad and listen to him share about his recovery.

As a young single person, I took great pride in deprivation, how I could survive and still look good. It seemed natural during the age of hippies and flower children, who were protesting the affluent, materialistic life of my parents' generation. Even though I carried the pain of my past with me, it was a time of positive growth for me, because I was loved and supported by the spiritual communities where I lived and worked. And it didn't take much money to live well.

When inflation hit in the mid-Seventies, I started getting credit cards. I discovered that a person had ninety days before the card company would threaten collection. I would pay the minimum due on one with a cash advance from another, allowing months to go by before I would have to pay anything out of pocket. Piling up this debt, I thought that somehow I was outsmarting the banks with my clever plan. This was how I acted out the deprivation and anxiety I felt. I was seeking a way out of my pain. I did whatever I could to relieve my enormous discomfort: sex, drugs, food, alcohol, trips to Europe, therapy and every conceivable workshop. I tried everything I could think of, but nothing fixed me. All this cost money, so I would charge it and worry about how to pay for it later.

My performance at work was suffering, and my job began falling apart. I left my job and the area. Either my mom or my new boyfriend would pay off my debts and bail me out of the tight spot I had created. In a short time the credit cards would all be up to their limits again. In 1984, I reached bottom, after one more move, one more emotionally abusive relationship, one more time of running up the cards, and one more job where the pain from my past affected my performance and relationships.

Panicked without a job, I turned to God for another test. If He was truly an abundant God, He would provide for me, even though I was down to my last $5.00 with no visible means of income. Sure enough, unexpected events brought money to me quickly. I decided to continue reaching out to this spiritual source and committed to go to meetings. The topic at my first meeting was "surrender." I remember hearing someone say she tried to have conscious contact with God during meditation, all she experienced was darkness and silence. She asked God to please speak up. During her day she had heard a clear voice say, "Be at Peace about this," referring to her current situation.

I left the meeting feeling good. One the way home, I stopped for gas. While standing there pumping gas, I saw two lottery tickets float down and land right by my feet. This surprised me. Just rubbish, I thought, or perhaps a sign from God? So I closed my eyes to meditate and ask God, "Am I supposed to buy a lottery ticket?" A very loud thought and a large number three came through my mind. It was so loud and clear that I was taken aback and asked, "How many do I buy?" Again a very loud thought and a large number three came through. Well, the third ticket I bought was significant, a real chance at the big spin, for millions of dollars. Now I was ready to surrender. With a million dollars dangling in front of my nose, I was ready to do whatever was suggested by my spiritual program. If any good was to come of this chance, I knew I had to stay connected to my Higher Power to make anything happen. So I did everything suggested: I got a sponsor, worked the Steps, read literature, and went to meetings.

While I was waiting for my chance at the big spin, a job offer came through that I really liked, but I had to fly to the facility for the training. All my expenses would be covered after I arrived. But I didn't have the plane fare. On my way to a meeting one night, I was really angry with God, because it seemed like nothing was happening. I demanded that He give me a sign that I would be okay. The deadline for buying the ticket for the training was the next morning, and I needed $150 by then or I wasn't going. If God really did not want me to go on this trip, I needed to know, some reassurance that I would be all right.

When I arrived at the meeting I was involved in setting up and completely forgot the ranting and raving I had done in the car. When it came time, I shared about my fear about not having a job. A woman I had never seen before indicated to me from across the room that she wanted to speak to me after the meeting. When she approached me, I saw that she was deeply moved by something. It kind of scared me. I couldn't imagine why my presence would be so moving to her. She asked me if I needed money. I was startled. What should I say? Yes? She then proceeded to write me a check for the exact plane fare amount. She was so grateful for how the program had worked in her life that she wanted to give back some of the abundance she had. She had tried a nonprofit organization to make a donation, but was unable to connect. "Okay God," she said, "Show me where this check should go." During my share, she heard a voice tell her, "That's the woman I want you to give the check to."

The day before the big spin, I got two letters, one was from the lottery saying I was not chosen and one from a church where I had made a donation. The church letter said that no matter what might be happening to me today, I can trust that God has only my greatest good in mind. Now I was on a new path of understanding; there is no reality in lack. I have learned that all things work together for good for me today. No matter what my fear, I know that fear is <u>F</u>alse <u>E</u>vidence <u>A</u>ppearing <u>R</u>eal.

The week before Christmas was my greatest gift of all, a spiritual awakening as promised on page 83 of the A.A. Big Book. The promises are part of what kept me coming back to meetings. I wanted the fear of people and of economic insecurity to leave me. My sponsor helped me to see the reason there was never enough money, time, food, or love to fill me was at the core of my deprivation— the abuse. From the moment I had agreed with my father that I deserved abuse, I was primed and conditioned for years of lack, abusive relationships, and jobs. My part was my tolerance for the abuse in my relationships and not doing what I needed to take good care of myself.

In a moment of clarity, I became aware of the insidious abuse in my current marriage. I made a new decision to say no to the abuse in my life. I knew from my Step work that I needed to make amends to my children and give them protection. It was empowering for me to give them what had not been given to me. I confronted my husband about his constant, abusive yelling and belittling of the kids. His abuse would not be tolerated any more. I explained to my two stepsons, who had not hugged me in five years, why I owed them amends. I assured them that to the best of my ability I would give them the protection they deserved. Their big brown eyes softened, and they gave me a big hug.

While taking a walk later that day, I was suddenly flooded with feelings of joy and peace at a level I had never experienced before. I realized that this experience must have been the spiritual awakening that is in the Twelfth Step. In the afternoon I had an appointment with a potential client with whom I had great difficulty securing a sale. When I met with her, she said that she had decided to turn all of her business over to me and wrote me a check for the largest sale I had ever closed in my life. In the ensuing months, twenty pounds fell off, and I felt more sane and solvent every day. Forty-three years of doing things my own way produced a failing business, three disastrous and sick marriages ending in divorce, and a lot of debt and pain. My failing business, which had come to a near standstill, was now starting to grow.

Working the Steps was like being launched on a path of learning about the greatest wealth of all—the abundance of unconditional love. Now, for me there is enough love, enough money, enough time, and best of all, *I am enough!*

I Am a Moneyaholic

He grew up and worked in a shadow.
In D.A. he learned to stand in the sun.

I am John and I am a Moneyaholic. Today, eleven and a half years after coming into Debtors Anonymous, I still can get paralyzed by the fear of losing what I presently have and fear not having enough for tomorrow. Yet my life has changed dramatically because of D.A.'s help, love and principles. Unlike so many who came from other programs, I had no idea I was acting out with money. I had no idea I had a problem or a disease, but then again everything in my life was perfect, if just this one deal would close. I had lived that way for many years and had no idea how my wife put up with it: a roller coaster business of ups and downs. Finally in her frustration, she suggested I go to her Al-Anon meeting. I, of course, went into denial, but I went anyway. It was the worst meeting in all creation. I hated it. However, during the meeting it was recommended to try six meetings before making up your mind about the program. So I did, and in one of those six meetings, someone talked about debting and this new program called Debtors Anonymous.

Mine is a story of extremes. I lived in a fantasy that because my family was very wealthy, I was wealthy. Now in some families that might be true, but my father's attitude has always been that what is yours is his, and what is his is his, meaning he had money and power and wasn't going to let go of it in any way. I lived and fantasized that because he had it, he would share it with me, if I played by his rules: Wrong. That was only one of the many illusions that brought me deep into debt. I had low self-esteem, and there were two ways to satisfy it: to impoverish myself on the one hand and binge on the other. Bingeing felt great in the moment. I liked the power of being able to buy everyone's dinner, flashing my gold card while saying "It's on me." I liked the rush of buying the best of whatever I wanted, always, while in the back of my mind thinking that if I got into trouble my father would bail me out: Wrong!

The disease of compulsive debting and spending has been with me from earliest childhood: acting out through stealing, lying and trying to impress people with what my father had accumulated. As the son of a powerful man, my low self-esteem was the feeling that I would never even live up to his shadow or stand in his footsteps. The feeling that I would never accomplish or be what he was led me deeper and deeper into self-pity. I tried to be smart, I tried to be a good negotiator, and most of all, I tried to get the best of people as I saw him do. It was not until years later in D.A. that I understood I was not meant to be my father. I was meant to be myself.

Both my father and mother lived as their immigrant parents had raised them—in fear of losing all they had. So, they never spent their money; they saved for tomorrow. The confusing part for me was how can people with so much money be so cheap? My mother lived in the past, my father in the future, and no one lived in the present. My father's classic line was: "Even Texaco can go bankrupt," meaning no matter how big and powerful you become, you can fail. That was my upbringing and training, so that was my foundation when I went out into the business world to build my career.

Until I was 28 years old, I worked for large corporations and never really had any problems with money. Although I started at trainee positions, being compulsive, I would work long and hard to impress the right people, always trying to get ahead. I was very successful at this. I lived in the psychological shadow of my father's affluence, thinking some day it would be mine, he would share it with me: Wrong. My father wasn't letting go of anything.

While I worked for corporations, I had a regular paycheck and mostly lived within my means. I began to acquire credit cards and lines of credit, just in case. After all, one never knew when there would be an emergency. Since I had good credit, bank after bank gave me credit lines and eventually one bank offered me a gold card, which in those days was really something. I had arrived. Life was great. I had a job. I dated constantly. I was always high, both literally and figuratively, without a care in the world. Being of a spiritual bent, I felt uncomfortable having so much when many friends had so much less. I was always helping out with loans by using my own lines of credit. In the beginning this worked. I would lend someone money; they would pay me back. It seemed good to me because I was helping a friend without sacrifice on my part. It looked good to the bank because I borrowed and paid it back, thus improving my credit standing, while my friends got the benefit of the money. Who knew about enabling at that time?

In 1979, I decided it was time to work for myself. I had spent too long making money for others. My ego was high; I felt I could do no wrong, and because I was spiritual, everything else in my life would just manifest. I lived between the extremes of low esteem and grandiosity. I lived in arrogance, separation and loneliness. So at the ripe old age of 29, I set out to create my career. My father offered to let me work for him. I thought that would be great, and I would be on my way to making millions: Wrong. My father, who works alone, was incredibly open in sharing his world, as long as I did not participate or threaten him in any way. It was okay for me to watch him work, but not to participate. I was not working for him like I thought, just watching. This escalated my feeling that he had the power. I felt impotent, not knowing how I would earn my next dollar, while watching him make a fortune. This went on for 18 months until I was able to find my first client and close a deal on my own. This deal led to a second, which led to a third. Before long, I was on my way to financial independence, so I thought.

During this period, it was psychologically devastating to watch my father make millions and not share it with me. In my mind, it belonged to me too. I would lull myself into a sense of false importance thinking that my presence was helping him, or I would pray for his deals to happen and think it contributed when they closed. It did not. He was self contained in his world, and I was nothing more than an ornament. My soul was hungry for love and willing to sacrifice my own needs, if only my father would just pay attention to me, rather than his quest for more money.

I had no idea at that time how much like my father I was, or how absorbed I was in proving to the world that I was not like him. But the horrible truth became apparent after I closed my first deal. I decided it was time for me to "do my own thing." Without telling my father, I searched for office space until I found it, and then told him I was moving out the next week: no notice, no explanation. What a great step of independence and freedom. The truth is I wanted his respect and admiration so much that I was becoming independent, saying no to being a puppet. I wanted to hurt him bad for not appreciating me.

Working for myself in this tiny little space was a great experience. Over the years I have had many offices, but I will always remember this one most fondly, because it was there my disease came to a head and my recovery began. I was on my own there with no source of income other than what I could create myself. I discovered the ebb and tide of cash flow. At this point my business started to take on a life of its own. Now my business had needs which I had to respond to. I had replaced enabling my father with enabling my business. My business became extremely demanding, always wanting new equipment and finding new ways for me to spend money. In addition, on my way to success, there were big power lunches, and keeping up with all the other mortgage brokers. Since I felt so much less than all of them, I needed more things to prove myself of their caliber.

This went on for quite a while until I reached the level of convincing the banks, based on the business I could bring to them, that they should make me a private banking client, even though I did not meet their financial criteria. Always being able to talk my way into situations, I got the bank to agree. Now I had my own office, a computer, a printer (they were much more expensive than today's computers and did far less), a complete telephone setup, and I was in private banking. This meant I had my own private banker who could lend me all the money I could ever want. I was in heaven, or so I thought. Little did I realize I was being set up for the fall. My ego felt I was God's gift to the business world, and I could do no wrong. I was fulfilling my self-appointed function of bringing spirituality into the business world.

One of the people that I dealt with needed to borrow $5,000 and would pay me back within a week. No problem. I wrote him a check from my line of credit account, and he had his money. Fifteen years later he has still not paid me back. The funny thing is he always promised to pay me the next week. I called him last year saying that I desperately needed some money, could he help me out, and he said he would once his next deal closed—I haven't heard from him since.

Next, I was involved with a business partner, and we were doing exotic deals with commodities, exports and imports. It was the ultimate drug—every deal meant that I would not only make millions, but lots of millions. Funny thing, with all the money and time invested, we never got a penny back. No deal ever closed, although many were only a day away. Always the promise and never the delivery. A smarter person would have learned by now, but not me, I was just getting going.

One day this business partner came to me and said he was about to lose his house and could I lend him some money? No problem. We were about to make millions, what was $20,000 anyhow among business partners? I can now admit how wonderful the false sense of power was; the feeling that I could affect other people was totally intoxicating. Now I had $25,000 out in lines of credit, and I was feeling very good that I could help so many others. In the meantime, my wife and I were living on a meager budget and just had enough to manage each week. I never used the lines of credit for my own pleasure; it was only to help others. I thought that would make it all right.

Now with my false ego flying, I was introduced to some clients who wanted to do a leveraged buyout of a supermarket chain. It didn't matter that I never had done one before; I would learn as I went along. Boy, did I end up learning! In the process of the leveraged buyout, certain fees were required to be advanced. I had advanced $25,000 on the promise of making hundreds of thousands in return for my clients who were busy traveling first class to Brazil in hopes of getting all the money together. Always the promise, and once again no delivery.

By the time this debacle was over, one of my clients went to jail for passing bad checks, and the other went bankrupt. I was left with another $25,000 in debt and nothing to show for it. One of the reasons I kept on putting good money after bad was that they were going to give me an Alaskan cruise once the deal closed. A big part of my disease was always looking for something for nothing. I could have traveled to Alaska first-class myself for the price this lesson cost me. So now I was $50,000 in debt with no one paying me back, and I was left to cover the monthly carrying costs along with my own and my business expenses.

Then I finally noticed a pattern occurring in my business deals. I would go from the depths of poverty to finally closing a deal, then have to pay off all the debt that I gotten into before the deal closed: Spend as if I still had the full amount and go back into deeper debt and anxiety, worrying about when the next deal would close. I would go from deal to deal hoping to be saved or rescued, just like so many others I had tried to rescue.

At that time there were less than seven D.A. meetings a week. I remember going to my first meeting and doing something I rarely did, I was silent for the whole meeting. I was in shock. I went to another meeting, and another, before I even opened my mouth. I couldn't believe that other people had similar issues or problems like mine. I was no longer all alone. After my fourth meeting, Robert J. suggested that I go for a cup of coffee with the group afterwards, and I was hooked.

Then my mind came up with every criticism in the book. I criticized everyone: They didn't really have the same problems I did; I made more money than they did, I had a larger debt, etc. But I kept on going to the meetings. In the beginning, I was able to go to three or four a week. I couldn't get over the concept that one could share their problems and their feelings without having someone else fix them. I was being allowed to have my feelings without anyone taking them away. It was not overnight, but somewhere after my first 90 days in the program, a dramatic change in my attitude took place and a change in the way I related to others.

I can honestly say that the recovery was not immediate, anything but. There I was doing my grandiose deals that were not producing any income. I had $50,000 in debt service I had to pay, plus my normal and regular bills. I was totally overwhelmed. I was ready for a Pressure Relief Group.

I had no idea what I was getting into. I still felt I was perfect and believed that if these clients had paid me back, I wouldn't have problems. I knew nothing about spending plans. I knew nothing about personal vs. business expenses. Boy, did I learn quick! I remember the pain of my first Pressure Relief Group man, asking me how much a month I spent on clothing. My answer was nothing, and his response was that a gentleman must spend at least $200 to $300 a month. I thought he was from another planet. What about massage? Flowers? Entertainment for me rather than for the business?

By the time my Pressure Relief Group was through with me I had a spending plan which took three meetings over the course of two weeks to formulate, with me kicking and screaming all the way. My Pressure Relief Group and I worked out a business and personal spending plan which I religiously followed, even though my Pressure Relief Group would break into laughter at my computer analysis of my monthly spending. There was something healing about entering my daily cash expenses into the computer. There was something very healing for me about recording a 50-cent purchase, when my mind had only thought in large numbers. I knew I had a problem when I kept on doing without personally so that I could buy a new piece of equipment for my business. I noticed that I used my business as the vehicle to get me into debt. Although I would not have enough money to buy a pair of slacks or a shirt, I could not understand the concept of having a business and a personal spending plan in which the personal spending came first. I always put the business first and then whatever was left over, if anything, went to me.

In my first spending plan, two-thirds of the total I spent went toward business expenses and one-third went toward personal expenses, and that was a real stretch. Today it is exactly the opposite: I spend two-thirds on my personal life and one-third on the business, thanks to the program. My Pressure Relief Group suggested that instead of only working on large deals and living a drama from paycheck to paycheck with lots of worry and fear in between, I should work on those smaller deals that I considered beneath me before D.A. They felt it was important to strive for balance in my business as well as my personal life.

That piece of advice changed everything. I started working on residential mortgages as well as commercial mortgages. Then over the years when the commercial market was active, the residential market was slow; when the commercial market was dead, the residential market was booming. Over and over again I followed my Pressure Relief Group's suggestions just on blind faith, and for me that faith sure paid off. However, I had not worked the First Step yet, i.e., admitted that my compulsive debting and spending had made my life unmanageable. But somewhere the love of my Pressure Relief Group and my original sponsor wore down my resistance, and I let go. Twelve years later, I can see how my life has been transformed through the love I received in the rooms. No one tried to fix me. I was accepted as I was, and that love transformed my life.

Although most people in the program got into trouble through their credit cards and therefore needed to rip them up, I did not. I needed credit cards for my business, and fortunately for me, my sponsor and Pressure Relief Group agreed. If they had told me I could not use a credit card in my business, I would not have stayed in the program; it was that simple. To this day, I tell newcomers that this is a very personal program. Everyone must find a recovery plan that works for them. However, I did cut up my personal credit cards when I shared at the meeting at St. Jeanne's one Monday night, and as I did, the love and support I felt were overwhelming. As for my business cards, what I did was prepay the bill. So if, for example, my average monthly bill was $500, I would prepay $500, so each month there was a credit balance. I would then prepay the next month the same way. That worked well for years, and then I changed to sending in a check when I had an expense. Now I just pay the bills as they come.

Within the first year I had experienced a major turnaround in almost every aspect of my life. It took a while, but even I could see that my life was getting better, because I was not the only one in control (HP). During that time I moved to a grander office on Fifth Avenue at Fifty-Sixth Street, which I was able to afford according to my spending plan. Miracle after miracle kept happening. Each time a money challenge appeared, after talking to my sponsor, so would the solution. My recovery, although dramatic, was still fragile, and I continued to go to three to four meetings a week, soaking in everything I could from the program. I started giving Pressure Relief Groups and sponsoring others until that too became compulsive. At this point my wife warned me that if I didn't spend more time at home, she was going to have an affair. I got the message real quick. This is a program of balance. We don't go from one extreme to the other, but strive to live debt free "one day at a time."

By the end of the second year, I had paid off the line of credit debts, but I was in trouble again, for without the pressure of debt over my head, I was available to have feelings. Although I was thrilled to reach the point where I had paid off my debts, I was also depressed, for in some weird way, my debts were very comforting to me. I am not sure I can explain why, but as long as I was indebted to someone, I was not responsible for making choices that benefit me. I talked about these feelings with my Pressure Relief Group, and they suggested I start saving money to experience what it would feel like to accumulate and not spend.

Until my Pressure Relief Group suggested I consolidate the bank accounts into one savings account, I would spread my money over many accounts, so I could never know how much I really had. Now I watched my savings grow in one account for a year. Each morning I would dial the bank on my computer hookup and just stare at my balance. For me it was like admiring a Rembrandt: something totally beautiful, yet out of my reach. I then very proudly went to my Pressure Relief Group and said I wanted to spend all this money to buy a new apartment. But, they suggested I let the money accumulate even longer and be aware of how it felt.

So I did. It brought up much deeper and more painful feelings than being in debt. Somehow I felt comfortable being in debt, because growing up I always felt like I owed my father for everything he gave me. I seemed bonded to the debting, for that's how I got his attention. Whenever he gave something, there would be such guilt and such strings attached to it that I would say to myself, "Some day I'll pay him back."

Somewhere in the second year of my recovery, I started writing three pages a day in a journal. I wrote my feelings or whatever happened in my life or was on my mind. I wrote two pages, then gave one page to the universe to write through me. I got some wonderful guidance that way. It was while writing that I came upon what I call a *Wish List:* a detailed list of all the material things I would like; a detailed list of the spiritual ideals I would like to attain; and a detailed list of the physical goals I wished to reach. I found separating the three categories very helpful. I continued going to meetings, having and giving Pressure Relief Groups, and making it a practice to make at least three program calls a day. I also took as many program calls as I could without interfering with my business. The program not only introduced me to the principles I live by, but also to many wonderful people with whom I have shared love and recovery.

Now, two years had gone by since my pressure people suggested I accumulate money to see how it felt. For someone who never allowed himself to have a feeling, it was both elating and frightening. I wanted to binge and get rid of it as soon as possible. With the help of the program, I had accumulated over $200,000 in cash, yet the funny thing was that I didn't feel prosperous. I remember always worrying: Would it be enough after taxes? Would it be enough to buy a house? Would I be able to keep up with the mortgage payments? Since I was always in fear of losing money, it became apparent to me that it didn't matter whether I was in debt or in prosperity: I got off on the excitement. So, I decided to call myself a Moneyaholic. I was addicted to money. Having it or not having it didn't make a difference. It was my drug of choice, with all the highs and lows that came with a drug.

Somewhere during that time I was asked to join the Board of the General Service Organization (GSO). D.A. was just six years old, and the GSO was also in its infant stages. Although we were knowledgeable about the great need for our program, we were still struggling with our growth. Then *The New York Times Sunday Magazine* printed an article about D.A., and overnight we were swamped with requests for help. Over the next couple of years, I became Treasurer, then Vice-Chairman. I was thrilled to give back some of what I had received. I personally believe that my recovery depends on my giving service anywhere I am called to do so.

I hope I have been able to share some of my transformation from grandiosity to poverty in the blinking of an eye to a person who has learned that my power comes from turning my will and my life over to the care of God as I understand God. For me recovery is a spiritual transformation. By consistently working the Steps, my life today is filled with love, good health, and a joy of knowing that although the disease may never go away, just for today, I am okay just the way I am.

Life definitely does get better after getting out of debt. One of the major changes that occurred within me was the perspective I had toward my accomplishments. From the program came a self-love and a respect which came from earning enough to pay for what I want and being responsible for having it.

I would like to share my secret about the house I live in. It took five years before one day I walked down the driveway and knew it was my house: I owned it; I paid the mortgage. I was just too frightened to take in the feelings of ownership.

Another magical thing happened as my recovery progressed. I learned to have compassion for others without trying to fix them or take away their feelings.

I also need to express that I was embarrassed for my financial success as my recovery continued. I believed that I would no longer be allowed in Debtors Anonymous if I wasn't in debt. I am one of many who can say there is life after debt, and since life is of our making, it has the potential to be wonderful. Today I have a wonderful house and gardens which give me tremendous pleasure. I know that garden is there, because I did the work of cleaning out the area, preparing the soil, planting the seeds, giving it the right nutrients, water and sunlight. After I did all that I was able to do, I turned it over and left it for Mother Nature to unfold her beauty. I have found one of the most helpful signs of my recovery is some days I just sit in my garden and take it all in. Sometimes I don't do any work, I relax and enjoy what is here and now. I am very proud of what I have in my life today, I have all the material possessions I could ask for. Surprise of surprises, I find I want less, not more, because one of the most subtle and most important discoveries in D.A. is that things can never satisfy the void. Satisfaction can only come from within. In the old days I would need more, because I was never able to be still enough to take in what I already had.

Over these last eleven years I have been able to help many compulsive debtors and have been helped in the process. I have noticed there are cycles to the disease, and just when we think we licked the desire to compulsively debt or spend, we get tested one more time. Debtors Anonymous saved my life, and I will always be grateful.

Recovery takes time. I have learned that for recovery to work, one must mentally accept one's new status. What happened to me when I first started to make money was it didn't conform to my low self-esteem image, the one that had to beg and scheme to get anything. I was used to scraps off the table, and now suddenly I was at the table as an honored guest. That was more than I could handle. The subconscious can only expand a little beyond its own mental image of itself. So if I feel I am worthy of making $100 dollars a day and someone offered me $1,000 a day, I would find some way to sabotage the experience.

I now know that one must prepare for wealth by setting goals and mentally conditioning the subconscious. This happens by the way I treat myself one day at a time. The principles of the program helped me feel worthy inwardly. It was not a question of how much money I spent on myself, but how much energy and time I spent with myself. The more I was aware of my feelings, the more connected to my Higher Power I became. That richness reflected in a better quality of life. For me, it meant saying no to a neurotic New York existence. Against all odds, I closed up my very fashionable New York office in a townhouse and moved it to a smaller town near my home. Most people thought I was crazy, but my decision came from peace of mind.

For the last three years I have worked in a country office eight minutes from my home where I found new opportunities. I do less and make more money, because I dramatically lowered my overhead while improving the quality of my life. The lesson I am working on now is to not have to prove myself to anyone. It's almost as if so much of what I have accomplished, I did to gain approval. I'd get more and more, and it just never seemed enough. The more I had, the more I wanted, and the more I feared losing what I had. It was my D.A. disease.

I don't know how it happened, I don't know when it happened, but somehow this compulsion was lifted. Day after day I became comfortable with what I had, so that today I feel like who I am. I have enough, and I do enough. And the miracle is that I appreciate my life.

Notes:

Notes:

Notes:

Notes:

Notes:

Notes:

Notes: